FINAL DAYS

Mark A. Finley

HART RESEARCH CENTER
FALLBROOK, CALIFORNIA

Edited by Ken McFarland
Cover art direction and design by Ed Guthero
Cover illustration by Nathan Greene

The author assumes full responsibility for the
accuracy of all facts, quotations, and references as
cited in this book.

ISBN 1-878046-34-9

Contents

For information about other spiritual resources available from Hart Research Center, call toll-free:

1-800-487-4278

Preface

A quiet hush fell over the audience. They sat spellbound as I graphically described Christ's suffering on the cross. During my appeal for surrender, some sat quietly with their heads in their hands; others knelt. Some meditated—others wept. Hearts opened to the Saviour! Sins were confessed—habits and attitudes surrendered! In gratitude to our loving Lord, they committed their lives to Him. Receiving His gift of eternal life, they became citizens of the kingdom. Jesus' promise, "a new heart also will I give you," (Ezekiel 36:26) became a reality.

In my evangelistic meetings over the last twenty years, I have witnessed thousands of people's lives transformed as they have met the Christ of the cross. At the cross, they have found forgiveness. At the cross, they have experienced a deeper love than they have ever known. At the cross, they have developed a sense of security. At the cross, their hearts have opened to receive a new source of spiritual power. Attitudes have changed! The bondage of habit patterns practiced for years has been broken. Jesus' words, "and I, if I be lifted up, will draw all men unto me," (John 12:32) have been literally fulfilled.

You, too, can experience the life-changing power of the cross. At the cross, you can receive His grace! His mercy and forgiveness are yours. His love breaks our hearts. Bloody nails, twisted thorns, and rough lumber have no power to save. But love does. Love is the strongest power in the universe. Christ's love revealed on the cross breaks hard hearts. It reawakens spiritual desires. As a breath of fresh air, it brings new life to the soul. As a cleansing bath, Calvary's love refreshes and revitalizes.

You may be a new Christian. This book is for you! It will lead you to appreciate God's love in a deeper way. Or you may have been a committed Christian for years. This book can bring new vigor and spiritual depth to your Christian experience. It is my prayer that you will relive the scenes of Calvary as you read these pages.

A familiar hymn raises the question, "Were you there when they crucified my Lord? Were you there when they nailed Him to the tree?" It is my prayer that as you journey through this book, you will be there to experience all that Calvary means.

—Mark A. Finley

1

The Face of Christ

The heat of southern and central India in June is absolutely stifling. When I stepped off a plane in Pune, I imagined myself stepping into a giant sauna. The temperature was 115 degrees in the shade. Gentle breezes were blowing, and almost immediately—within seconds—beads of sweat stood out on my forehead and began running down my face. My shirt stuck to my body, and I had to keep separating it and waving it to let a little breeze through.

John Wilmont, a ministerial colleague and my host, met me. As he and I traveled together, we came into a Hindu village. On our way through the village, John said to me, "Mark, I have held an evangelistic series here, and I want to take you to meet a lady who came to my meetings. You will be amazed at this woman. She was a Hindu and became a Christian—and the light of Christ shines in her life."

We drove along a dirt road to a small hut. The hut was probably six feet wide and eight feet long, with a thatched roof, mud walls, and no furniture at all inside except for a mat.

As we got out of the car, an older woman with deeply etched lines in her face and long, flowing hair came out of the hut, her hands trembling. But it was her eyes that attracted me—dark eyes that just sparkled. We could not speak the same language, but I knew she was a sister in Christ.

She gestured to me to come in, so, bending low, I entered her home on my hands and knees, crawling into her little hut. A flickering light illuminated the darkness. I could see the mat on the floor, and in the dim light, I saw something also on the wall. My eyes were attracted to it immediately. There on the wall was a picture of Jesus. Her hut was profoundly simple, yet simply profound—a mat on the floor and a picture of Jesus on the wall!

As we sat there in the hut unable to communicate, she spoke in the beautiful Urdu language. She kept motioning with a smile toward the picture on the wall, and her face reflected not only the flickering light of the room but the face of Jesus Himself. The face of Christ and the beauty of His glory, reflected in her face, confirmed the fact that we were brother and sister in Christ.

> "For God, who commanded the light to shine out of darkness, hath shined in our hearts, to give the light of the knowledge of the glory of God in the face of Jesus Christ." 2 Corinthians 4:6.

If you want to know what God is like, look into the face of Jesus Christ. If you desire to know God, look into the face of Jesus. The light of God's glory, the splendor of God's majesty, shines in the face of Jesus.

We have no artist's depiction of what Jesus' face looked like. The pictures of Jesus we commonly see today are mere products of the artist's imagination. True, a few representations of Jesus are found in centuries-old catacombs, but nothing in ancient literature or art clearly reveals what Christ looks like. We have no Polaroid snapshot of the face of Christ. We really don't know the contour of His face, the length or color of His hair, the color of His eyes. We can only surmise.

Maybe the reason for that is that our Lord desires us to look at other aspects of His face. Maybe there is something more important than the physical features of the face of Christ. What does the Bible really teach us about the face of Christ? What inspiration can we gain by looking into His face?

Let's consider five aspects—five glimpses—of the face of Christ:

1. The shining face.
2. The steadfast face.
3. The soiled face.
4. The suffering face.
5. The smiling face.

What do we see when we look into the face of Christ? What does His face reveal? What pictures of the face of Christ does the Bible give us?

First, it presents His shining face—a face aglow with the glory of God. Away from the hustle of the crowd, away from the crowded city streets of Jerusalem, away from the press and the throng of human life, away from the hectic activity, away from the frantic pace, Jesus steals away to pray.

"And after six days Jesus taketh Peter, James, and

John his brother, and bringeth them up into an high
mountain apart. And was transfigured before them
[The word *transfigured* means changed—changed
from the earthly to the supernatural, transformed.
Something happened to Jesus.]: and his face did
shine as the sun, and his raiment was white as the
light. And, behold, there appeared unto them, Moses
and Elias talking with him." Matthew 17:1-3.

In that mountain retreat all alone in the quiet-
ness, away from the hustle and bustle of the crowd,
Jesus' face, as He communed with His Father, shone
as the sun. Before Jesus lay betrayal, ridicule, mockery, nails, the spear, the crown of thorns—and the
cross. Before Him lay agony, suffering, loneliness,
discouragement, and death. But away from the
hustle and bustle of the crowd, away from the strain
of life's intense activity, in one-to-one communion
in prayer with the Father, His face shone as the sun.

His shining face calls us from the intense activities of life. His shining face calls us from the stress
and strain of life. His shining face calls us from our
rush and hurry. His shining face calls us to quiet-
ness, meditation, and prayer.

Moses and Elijah came especially to answer Jesus'
prayer. Some who read this passage may ask, "Is
this some incarnation of Moses and Elijah?" They
read this passage and wonder what was going on.
According to the Bible, Moses died without ever entering the Promised Land. His dreams and hopes
were not realized. He had led the children of Israel
in the Exodus for years, yet his own hopes were
dashed. He looked into the Promised Land but never
entered it. Instead, he died. But the Lord did ex-
ceedingly, abundantly above what Moses could ever
ask or think, because Christ came down and con-
tended with Satan, according to the book of Jude,
over the body of Moses. And according to the book

of Deuteronomy, Moses' body was searched for and never found. Our Lord resurrected Moses from the dead and took him to heaven.

So Moses, who died and went into the grave and then came out, came to Jesus at the point of His death to give Him encouragement and the assurance that, although He would go into the grave, He too would come out.

And Elijah, the one who never saw death—the one who ascended to heaven in a flaming chariot—also came to encourage Jesus. The very encouragement Jesus needed—the precise instruction and hope He needed—came in an answer to prayer. I wonder just what Moses and Elijah said to Jesus.

You know, the Bible actually records something about that conversation. What did Moses and Elijah say to Jesus? How did they encourage Him? What hope did they bring to Him there alone, away from the crowd, in the quiet place of prayer? Jesus' face shines as the sun—it reveals the iridescent glory of God. Before Him is betrayal, suffering, trial, agony, and death. But as Jesus prays, God sends Moses and Elijah. This is no reincarnation; it is literally Moses resurrected from the dead who comes down from heaven. It is literally the very Elijah who ascended to heaven without dying who comes down from heaven. What do they say to Jesus?

> "And, behold, there talked with him two men, which were Moses and Elias: Who appeared in glory, and spake of his decease [His death or His departure] which he should accomplish at Jerusalem." Luke 9:30, 31.

They came and spoke about His departure. The New Testament was written in the Greek language, and the Greek word for "departure" or "decease" is *exodus*. An exodus is a journey into the unknown.

Jesus was going to take an exodus—an exodus through Pilate's judgment hall, an exodus up Calvary's mountain, an exodus leading to a cross, an exodus that—because of the sins of the human race—would lead to the hiding of the Father's face, an exodus from life and into darkness.

Jesus was about to journey into the domain of death without the conscious assurance of His Father's presence. Would He be separated from the Father forever? Would the fellowship and love they had enjoyed from eternity be gone forever? Jesus was going to go on an exodus, and Moses—one who had already been on just such an exodus—came to give Him encouragement and hope. "Jesus," he must have said, "if You die and go into the grave and come out again, thousands—when You come again—will be resurrected."

And Elijah must have said, "Lord, if You go to the cross and unyieldingly and unflinchingly face the enemy, thousands will never die, because when You come again, they will be resurrected and go to heaven."

Jesus obtained courage for His exodus—His journey into the unknown. Away from life's hustle and bustle, its clatter and clamor, its loud voices, Jesus—in the quiet place of prayer and with His face shining as the sun—found strength for His exodus.

Each of us is on our own exodus, for life itself is a continuing journey into the unknown. One telephone call at any time could change our lives. One phone call from a father or a mother, telling us that they need an operation. One phone call from a son or a daughter. One phone call from school administrators.

One visit to a doctor could change your whole life. Or one winding curve on an icy road in the black of night. We don't know what's before us. We don't know the trials, the temptations, ahead. Satan prepares his temptations and sets his traps to lead us into trouble. He studies the genetic predisposition of each personality. He knows where your father was weak, where your mother was weak, where your grandfather was weak, and, following that genetic line, he knows where you have indulged certain thought patterns for years and where certain repeated habit patterns have become part of life. All of that is part of Satan's strategy, and he plans for you temptations and insidious, hellish deceptions to lead you into sin. He plans to chain you in bondage. What lies ahead of you and me is the unknown.

But before Jesus launched out into the unknown and before He journeyed on His exodus through trial, betrayal, and loneliness, He quietly received strength. From God, He received power for the journey. The way to face the test is to prepare for it before it comes. The way to face temptation is to get ready for it before temptation comes.

Amid the hectic strains of late-twentieth-century living, amid the rush of life, the shining face of Jesus calls us to prayer. His shining face calls us to devotion. His shining face calls us to quiet moments with God at times when up seems down and down seems up. When our heads are spinning and life is in a whirl and there are a million things to do, His shining face calls to devotion. He came down from the mountain, and as He did, He was filled with the presence of God.

"It came to pass when the time was come that he should be received up, he steadfastly set his face to go to Jerusalem." Luke 9:51.

The steadfast face. I like that word—*steadfast*. Nothing wishy-washy about it—no spineless jellyfish here. "He steadfastly set his face." He would be stripped to the waist. His hands would be tied above his head. Strong-armed Roman soldiers with leather whips in which were embedded pieces of steel and bone would rip large shreds of flesh out of His back. The Roman whip could even be wrapped around its victim and pull out inner organs of the abdomen if the whipping were continued for long.

He faced the scourging; He faced the crown of thorns. He faced the agony of the nails; He faced the gory ordeal of the cross. And Christ did not flinch. He steadfastly, firmly fixed His eyes on the cross. Steadfastness—hanging in there when times get tough—is a quality of biblical heroes.

Rejected by his society, Noah steadfastly banged nails for 120 years. Joseph, sold out by his brothers, betrayed and wrongly condemned by Potiphar, then cast into prison, steadfastly hung in there and did not give up. The captive Daniel had all his hopes smashed and saw all his dreams dancing away like a shadow, like grains of sand slipping through the fingers, like a bottle thrown at the wall and dashed into a thousand pieces, yet he "purposed in his heart" to serve God.

Now and again someone says to me, "You know what happened to me? It is so terrible. So and so said this about me, and I am not going to come to church anymore. It is just so *bad* what those people are saying about me. I have been condemned unjustly."

I point you to Joseph, condemned unjustly. Steadfastness means that you hang in there. Looking into the face of Christ, I receive courage. Looking into the face of Christ, I see stalwartness. Looking into the face of Christ, I hang in there.

True, the church may have its problems—its difficulties. There are many dropouts today—people who drop out of Christianity because of the way other Christians have treated them. People drop out of Christianity because things did not go their way, and they say, "Lord, where were You when my child was sick? Lord, if You are so good, why did my marriage go through that conflict?"

Yes, there are a lot of dropouts today, but looking into the face of Jesus, we see that He faced trial, so we can face trial. He faced betrayal, so we can face betrayal. He faced ridicule, so we can face ridicule. He faced physical suffering, so we can face physical suffering. He faced abuse, so we can face abuse. Looking into the steadfast face of Jesus, we have courage.

I think of Carol—one of the most athletic, ambitious kids you ever saw. Eighteen years old, full of life, she loved swimming, softball, and motorcycles. Now, it is rather unusual for an eighteen-year-old girl to jet around on a motorcycle, but Carol was full of life.

Coming around a corner one day, she wiped out her motorcycle. The wheels went out from under her, and she damaged her leg severely. The only choice the physicians had was to amputate her leg, so they did, just above the knee. When her dad heard about the accident, he was away meeting some speaking appointments. Dr. Schuller came home to find his daughter, Carol, in the hospital. Her leg had been amputated, and he had feared the worst. Standing before her bed, he took her hand in his, looked into her eyes, and began to feel at the sheet. Instantly, he knew—no leg.

He looked her in the eyes. "Carol, it is gone, isn't it?"

"Dad," she replied, "you have always told me, 'If

there is a mountain, go over it; if there is a mountain, go around it; if there is a mountain, dig a tunnel through it. If you can't go over the mountain and you can't go around the mountain and you can't dig a tunnel through it, keep digging in your mountain, and you will find gold.' Dad, you have always told me that, and I am going to steadfastly hang in there with Jesus."

For seven weeks, Carol lay in the hospital. She was fitted with an artificial leg and began to walk on it.

"Dad," she said, "I want to play softball."

"Carol, you've got an artificial leg," Dr. Schuller reminded her. "You can't play softball."

"Dad, I still have my softball uniform," she answered, ignoring his protests. "I am putting it on, and I am going to try out for the girls' team."

So Dr. Schuller drove her down to the softball field. He couldn't bear to watch his daughter. She walked with a terrible limp. Just before she got out of the car, he looked at her and said, "Carol, how in the world are you going to play softball with an artificial leg? Carol, look, you can't even run."

She smiled and said, "Dad, I have that all figured out. When you hit home runs every time, you don't have to run very fast." That is steadfastness!

When the trials of life come, when heartaches come, by looking into the face of the Master—looking into the face of the living Christ, looking into the face of the One who suffered ridicule and mockery and physical pain and abuse—we develop that quality of Christian life called steadfastness.

The shining face calls me to prayer—it calls me away from the hectic activities of life. The steadfast face calls me to courage—it calls me to hang in there when things don't go well. The shining face . . . the steadfast face . . . and now, the soiled face.

Come with me to a garden called Gethsemane and see the earth-stained face—the soiled face. The world trembles in the balance. Jesus, alone in Gethsemane, prays again. "And he went a little further, and fell on his face, and prayed." Matthew 26:39. He fell on His face—face down in the dirt.

"O my Father, if it be possible, let this cup pass from me: nevertheless not as I will, but as thou wilt." The soiled face—the earth-stained face. Jesus' natural inclinations called one way, but His duty called the other way. Did Jesus have a will of His own? What does the text say? "Not as *I will,* but as thou wilt." So He had a will of His own.

Did Jesus, in His own natural will, look forward to going to the cross? Did He look forward to betrayal? Did He look forward to the ridicule and the nails? Could He really experience loneliness and heartache, or was He immune from all that? Could Jesus really experience physical suffering? Did the nails really hurt Him? Did He really go through agony?

If you had asked Jesus, "Do You choose the cross in Your own human will? Are You looking forward to it?" what do you think He would have said? Undoubtedly, He would have answered, "Not at all. I personally do not look forward to the cross. My human nature leads me away from the cross, not toward it."

But Jesus surrendered His will and said, "Not as I will, but as thou wilt." My Christian life is a matter of day by day choosing God's will and not my will. And when I am impatient, when I want to lash out, I sense that my carnal nature—my selfish will—is in the ascendancy. Then, from the depths of my soul, I look into the soiled face of Jesus, and I say, "Lord, I choose Your will."

Christianity is manifest when my choices and God's choices are obviously and evidently the same, not when my choices and God's choices are different. Let me give you an example.

I have never smoked in my life. It is no test of my Christianity today not to smoke cigarettes—no test at all. Since I have not smoked all my life, that is not a test for me, though it may be a test for somebody else. I am sure it is a test for many, many people. So there is no conflict between my will and God's will over that issue.

But suppose that over some other issue or decision, I believe myself to be in the right, and I argue for my position stubbornly, selfishly, arrogantly. And the question is, "Mark, are you willing to surrender your will to the living Christ?" The soiled face calls me from what I want to do, to what God wants me to do.

In your own life, is there anything you are doing that you really want to do, but that you know in your heart of hearts is not right—that it is wrong? The soiled face leads you to say with Jesus, "Not my will be done, but Your will be done." This is the essence of Christianity. We have a new Lord, and the Lord who lives in our heart, the Lord who sits on the throne of our life, is King, and His will is supreme.

The shining face calls me to prayer. The steadfast face calls me to courage. The soiled, earth-stained face calls me to surrender my will—my weak, trembling, feeble, egotistical will—day by day in the quiet place of prayer. Looking into His soiled face, His earth-stained face, I surrender my will to Him.

Consider next the suffering face. They stripped Him to the waist. They tied Him to a single pole in a moonlit courtyard with the stars twinkling overhead in the heavens. Strong-armed Roman soldiers approached Him with their whips and lashed His back. With clenched fists, they struck Him in the face. "And when they had blindfolded him, they struck him on the face, and asked him, saying, 'Prophesy, who is it that smote thee?'" Luke 22:64.

Notice again the abuse Jesus suffered. "Then did they spit in his face, and buffeted him; and others smote him with the palms of their hands." Matthew 26:67. They spat on the face of the Son of God—the face of the One worshiped by ten thousand times ten thousand angels, the face of the One at whose very name these angels winged their way to worlds afar, the face of the One to whom for millennia they had sung, "Holy, Holy, Holy." They spat on the lovely, beautiful face of Jesus.

The Bible says, "They did spit in his face, and buffeted him." "Buffeted him" means that they slapped Him in the face. "Others smote him with the palms of their hands." The suffering, smitten face—black eyes, bloodied nose, swollen lips—the face of the Son of God abused.

Who is this whom they strike? Who is this who suffers so? Who is this who endures such agony? Who is this with the blackened eyes and the bloody face? It is Jesus, the divine Son of God. Puny men, created by the living God, approach the Creator and strike Him in the face. Cursing and swearing, they mock Him.

In a sense, I was there, you were there, all mankind was there. We were there that night in the shadows in Pilate's courtyard. We stepped forward that night, and with our hands, we slapped Him in the face. You say, "Oh, I wasn't there. The Romans did that. The Jews put Him up on the cross; they consented to His death. I wasn't there."

But, in a sense, we were all there that day in Pilate's

judgment hall. In a sense, we were all there when they put the nails through His hands. Because every departure from right and every deed of cruelty brings sorrow to His heart.

When I know better and I consciously, willingly turn my back on Him today, I bring grief to Him. When I know better and I am dishonest, when I know better and I consciously, willingly lie, when I know better and I lose my temper and get angry, when I know better and lustful thoughts dominant my mind, when I know better and willingly, consciously rebel against Him, I bring Him grief. I bring Him sorrow. I bring Him heartache. The One who loves me so, the One who endured the suffering on the cross so I wouldn't have to suffer eternally, suffers still when I rebel against Him.

So in the shadows, I come to that cross, and I see men and women striking Him in the face. And looking into that bloody face, I say, "Oh, Lord, I lay down my weapons of warfare. I surrender everything I have and everything I am, to You. I want to bring joy to Your heart, not sorrow."

The shining face calls me to prayer. The steadfast face calls me to courage. The soiled face calls me to surrender. The suffering face calls me to lay down anything that separates me from Him.

But there is also a smiling face. The Bible starts with a perfect world and ends with a perfect world. In its first two chapters, the Bible begins with no suffering or sickness or death, and in its last two chapters, it ends with no suffering or sickness or death. One day there will be a new society—a new heaven and a new earth. One day the River of Life will flow from the throne of God again. One day the Tree of Life will bear its fruit again. "And there shall be no more curse: but the throne of God and of the Lamb shall be in it; and his servants shall serve him:

And they shall see his face." Revelation 22:3, 4.

One day He shall come again, not as a babe in Bethlehem's manger, but as a King; not wearing a crown of thorns, but a crown of glory; not with nails through His hands, but carrying a scepter in His hands; not as a servant, but as a Master. One day He shall come again as King of kings and Lord of lords. One day sickness and sin and suffering will be over. One day the earth will be illuminated with the glory of God, and a knowledge of the Lord will cover the earth as the waters cover the sea. One day His name will be on every tongue, every knee shall bow, and every tongue shall confess that He is Lord. One day the glory of God will fill the earth again, and one day we shall see His face.

Because of that hope, we can endure the temporary sorrows of life. Because of that hope, we can endure the heartache and suffering in the world we live in. One day we shall see His face. I love the way the poet puts it:

I don't look back; God knows the fruitless efforts,
The wasted hours, the sinning regrets.
I leave them all with Him who blocks the records
And mercifully forgives and forgets.

I don't look forward; God sees all the future.
The road that's short or long will lead us home
And He will face with me its very trial
And bear with me the burdens that come.

I don't look around me; then fears assail me
So wild the tumult of earth's restless seas,
So dark the world, so filled with woe and evil,
So vain the hope of comfort or of ease.

I don't look within me; for I am the most wretched,
My self has naught on which to stay my trust.
Nothing I see, save failure and shortcomings

And weak endeavors crumbling into dust.

So, I don't look back; I don't look forward;
I don't look around me; I don't look in,
But I look up into the face of Jesus,
For there my heart can rest; my fears are stilled.

There is joy, and love, and light for darkness,
And perfect peace for every hope fulfilled.

In the rush of life, I look into His shining face, and He calls me to prayer. When I am about ready to give up, I look into His steadfast face, and He calls me to courage. When my will and my desires conflict with His, I look into His soiled face, and He calls me to surrender. And when openly and willingly, I turn my back on Him, I look into His suffering face and kneel in repentance. And finally, when down seems up and up seems down, when the road is long and the journey is tough, when obstacles fill the way and my life is broken, I look into the smiling face of Jesus Christ, and the hope of His return spurs this pilgrim on!

2

Three Men Meet Jesus

On the darkest Friday in all history, three men meet Jesus. The first meets Him as He struggles—stumbling beneath the weight of an enormous cross—along the path to the mount called Calvary. When Jesus falls to the path in exhaustion, His cross is placed on the brawny shoulders of another.

A second man meets Jesus while hanging at His side on a cross of his own. But before breathing his last, he finds new hope and life in the Saviour's assurance of salvation.

The third meets Jesus while standing in Roman armor at the foot of the cross. As he witnesses Christ's dying agonies and hears His words of forgiveness, the stern heart of the centurion is broken, and he cries out in conviction, "This man is the Son of God!"

These three men came from widely diverse backgrounds. Their life experiences—and their ways of viewing things—were certainly not the same. Yet they shared one thing in common: When each met Jesus, he was never the same again.

Join me in considering these three:

1. **Simon**, a hard-working African farmer—**the Compelled One.**

2. **The thief**, a rebellious Judean youth—**the Crucified One.**(See Luke 23:39-43.)

3. **The Roman centurion**, a hardened military officer—**the Callous One.**

Simon: The Compelled One

The Scriptures describe Simon in one brief text: "And as they came out, they found a man of Cyrene, Simon by name: him they compelled to bear his cross" Matthew 27:32.

Who was this man? Scripture called him "a man of Cyrene." His home was in North Africa. He had arrived after a long, arduous journey to Palestine. He followed the dusty roads of Libya, trekked the sandy pathways across the valley of the Nile, passed the rocky coasts of the Mediterranean, and crossed the highlands through the wilderness of Judea, arriving at last in Jerusalem.

Simon's sons were believers in Jesus. Scripture gives us their names—Alexander and Rufus (see Mark 15:21). According to one great classic on the life of Christ, "Simon had heard of Jesus. His sons were believers in the Saviour, but he himself was not a disciple."—*The Desire of Ages*, p. 742.

Notice again the words of Matthew 27:32: "They found a man of Cyrene, Simon by name: him they compelled to bear his cross."

To compel is to forcibly press someone into service. The word here in the original language is a military term meaning to commandeer—it implies a strict order. He was *drafted*—conscripted into service. He had no choice in the matter. He was forced—coerced.

Picture the scene. Simon rounds a sharp corner on a narrow, cobblestone Jerusalem street and finds himself face to face with a jeering mob. He is swept up in the crowd and carried along as if by a wave of the sea. The Roman soliders force the Son of God through the mass of shouting people. Weary, suffering, weak from the loss of blood following two Roman lashings, Jesus falls in exhaustion at Simon's feet. He can no longer go on.

Simon recalls the discussions his own sons have had about this man, and as he looks into the innocent eyes of Jesus, his soul is suddenly flooded with compassion.

To look at Jesus is to see all too clearly the ordeal He has been through. All through a sleepless night, He has been shuttled from one leader to another: from Annas to Caiaphas, then to Pilate, and from Pilate to Herod. He has had nothing to eat or drink. He has been scourged, spat upon, and crowned with thorns from which blood still flows freely. Simon recoils from the scene in horror. His facial expression indicates his sympathy and compassion for this man.

Before he realizes what is happening, he hears the words, "Hey, you there! Yes, you." Strong arms grasp him. The cross is thrust upon his shoulders. "Walk on," he is ordered. "Carry the cross." Had Simon arrived five minutes sooner, he would have missed the crowd. Five minutes later, and the procession would have passed. But because he arrived when he did, he is forced to carry the cross. Fair? Hardly. But as many note, life often doesn't seem fair.

Simon seizes the cross and carries it with dignity. In that cross he will find his life's greatest blessing. The cross was the means of his salvation, the source of his reconciliation to his Creator.

"The bearing of the cross to Calvary was a great blessing to Simon, and he was ever after grateful for this providence. It led him to take upon himself the cross of Christ from choice, and ever cheerfully stand beneath its burden."—*The Desire of Ages*, p. 742.

It doesn't seem fair that Simon should have been forced to carry a cross that was not even his own— that he should have been rudely detained from whatever mission had brought him to Jerusalem, to assist in an execution. For Simon, what happened that day was not fair. And neither is life fair for you and me today. The anguished questions arise continually:

"Why was my father killed when I was a child?"

"Why did my husband leave me?"

"Why was I brought up in a home with conflict?"

"Why am I out of work?"

Life is not fair, but God is fair! Simon found—in the injustices, unfairness, and inequities of life—life's greatest blessing.

For Simon, the old skull-faced mountain no longer scowled; it was now the smile of God to his soul.

Some of us today, like Simon, are conscripted and compelled to carry crosses not of our choosing. Rapidly changing circumstances thrust us into little-imagined difficulties. A job change, a career change, or other sudden events thrust circumstances upon us as a cross.

❑ Financial setbacks

❑ Illness

❑ Straying children

❑ Work-related stress

❑ Marital problems

❑ Loneliness

❑ Loss of a job

❑ Pressures of single parenthood

The demands seem too heavy, the load too great. Yet, as someone has said:

> "Every trial is a call to prayer,
> Every burden a bridge to the Saviour,
> Every difficulty an invitation to our knees."

What crosses have been thrust upon your shoulders? I am not suggesting that a cross is only good. We must see in the cross of Calvary the result of evil. This is reflected in our personal crosses. These crosses Satan often thrusts upon our shoulders in an effort to destroy us. Yet God takes the horror, evil, wickedness, and malignity of the cross and turns it into an agency for our salvation.

Seize your cross! Carry it with dignity. Walk through life, not with a martyr complex, but as a triumphant conqueror. For in the end, the crosses of life that we are compelled to bear become life's greatest blessing. In the very process of joyfully accepting circumstances we cannot change, we enter into some of life's greatest joys.

Once a biologist watched as an ant carried a piece of straw. Since the straw was much bigger than the ant and many times its weight, the little creature struggled under the load. Struggled, that is, until he came to a large crack in the earth. There he dropped his straw, and the burden became a bridge!

Let Christ transform you from within.
Let your BURDENS become BRIDGES.
Let your TRIALS become TRIUMPHS.
Let your SCARS become STARS.
Let your CROSSES become CALVARYS, where you meet God.

Three men met Jesus: Simon, the Compelled One, met Him under the crushing load of a heavy burden. Perhaps that is where you, too, will meet Him.

The Penitent Thief: The Crucified One

The second man to meet Jesus that day was the dying thief on the cross. What was his background? Evidently he was a companion of Barabbas. Barabbas claimed to be the Messiah. He claimed authority to set things right and establish a new political order. He went so far as to declare that whatever he could get by theft or robbery was his.

The young man dying on the cross accepted this false messiah. He had accepted an illusion; he had grasped at a phantom. There are many such illusions in life—many false messiahs incapable in themselves of providing deep, inner satisfaction. Money, pleasure, academic degrees, power, position, prestige—all fall short when it comes to meeting the needs of the soul.

The thief was a Jew for whom religion didn't satisfy, who sought freedom but came up empty-handed. He was a seeker who sought answers in all the wrong places. He had probably heard Jesus preach. But His careless attitude toward religion led him to compromise. He and his buddies became more daring.

I perceive him as a good boy gone bad. He watched as Jesus healed the sick. He beheld, amazed, as He multiplied the loaves and fishes.

The thief had no doubt been brought up in a conservative Jewish home. He attended rabbinical schools. He kept the Sabbath and meticulously followed laws of health. Religion was an external form. And his cynical attitude toward religion led him to pursue his own selfish interests. Life was filled with fun. Each day was another opportunity to have a good time.

He and his buddies became more daring. Simple routine no longer held any excitement. The law stood as a challenge. He and his companions defied its restrictions.

Soon the long arm of Roman law reached for him. He was arrested, jailed, tried, found guilty, and condemned to death. And now he was being executed. There was no escape.

As blood dripped from those nail wounds, he couldn't pull his hands or legs free and walk away. This was for real. The stench of death was in the air. He couldn't move, because it hurt too much. Suddenly it dawned upon him—he was going to die!

Guilt—a gnawing inner discomfort, a sense of being off balance, a sense that everything was not right between himself and God—seized his entire being.

In those final moments, the penitent thief cried out, "Lord, remember me!" Never has that plea gone unanswered. There in those last moments, amidst his suffering, peace flooded into his soul. His sins were forgiven. Beyond the pain, he had the assurance of heaven at last. Yet we see him again.

The Roman soldier broke the legs of the thieves and then carried them away. Gehenna was outside the city. It was a perpetually burning garbage dump. With legs broken, the thieves were dragged away by some donkey and thrown on a rubbish pile. Yet bright gleams of hope penetrate that darkness. The

Saviour's promise cheered the thief in his dying hour.

A dying thief found forgiveness; you can find it, too. The thief's problem was guilt. Guilt is the sense of inner condemnation which comes from being out of harmony with God. Accusing voices plague the conscience. The dying thief wondered, "Is there any hope for me?"

In March of 1992, I held a series of evangelistic meetings in Moscow's Kremlin auditorium. After one of the meetings, I was seated in my little office, when the door suddenly flung open. A tough-looking young man with a scruffy beard and rough appearance came bursting into the room. Believing he was going to attack me, I stepped back. My Russian translator stepped between us. Immediately the man began waving his arms and talking animatedly in Russian.

My translator explained that this man was one of Moscow's notorious criminals. He had been in and out of jail twenty-eight times. Filled with guilt and hopeless about his future, he longed to find peace. I calmly read 1 John 1:9: "If we confess our sins, he is faithful and just to forgive us our sins." I told him the story of the thief on the cross who found forgiveness.

Jesus is the same Saviour today. He offers forgiveness. He offers deliverance. He offers salvation. Take it! Rejoice in it! Praise God for it!

With tears running down his face, this guilty young Russian knelt and received God's forgiveness. The guilty thief—a young man who had consistently compromised and made wrong choices, found in Jesus his last fleeting ray of hope. Nailed to the cruel cross, dying as a condemned criminal, he desperately reached out to Jesus.

Only one death-bed repentance is recorded in the Bible—this story of the thief who turned to Jesus while on his cross.

Someone has said, "One to give us hope and only one to keep us from presuming on God's mercy."

The poet, describing the death of a man falling from his horse, wrote:

"Somewhere between the stirrup and the ground, mercy I sought, and mercy I found."

Mercy is still available! The dying thief found in the loving heart of God that it was safe to come home.

Three men meet Jesus: One meets Him ascending a hill. Another meets Him hanging by His side. Still another meets Him standing at His feet. All meet Him and are changed.

The Roman Centurion: The Callous One

It was a *violent age,* in a *violent land,* among a *violent people*—and he was a *violent man.* The Roman solder was a hard-hearted, callous, rough, tough fighter. He was a solder of fortune always on guard for the unexpected ambush. He handled people roughly. He was truly an unlikely prospect for the gospel. As superintendent of executions and a professional killer of criminals, his heart was hardened against any religious thought.

Friday morning, he received orders to carry out the crucifixion (execution). "Let's be on with it—let's be done with it!"

This wasn't the first time he had supervised an execution, and it wouldn't be the last—or would it be?

"Move over, you weeping women!" he shouted. "Step aside, you jeering priests! You, there, Mister! Get back!"

The Scripture calls him a centurion—the commander of 100 men. He was amazed that Jesus offered no resistance. Christ's suffering only revealed His kingly glory. He submitted to the nails without flinching; He lay down without a struggle. As the cross was lifted and plunged with great violence into the hole prepared for it, no cursing proceeded from His lips—only a prayer.

A little of the Roman centurion is in us all. Defensively, we debate to protect our little kingdoms.

As he watched Jesus' loving disposition toward His enemies, the centurion exclaimed, "Truly, this was the Son of God."

Something about Jesus attracted his attention. The look of pain gave way to serene trust. Each time Jesus moved His head on the rough cross, the wooden bar pressed the thorns more deeply into His forehead, but He uttered no word of complaint. The nails tore ever-widening, gaping holes in His hands and feet, yet no curses flowed from His lips!

The Roman centurion listened as the Saviour prayed, "Father, forgive them." As he beheld the drama unfolding before him, something was pulling the centurion out of himself. He was being drawn to this man. There were god-like qualities in this Jesus. The centurion may have recalled Pilate's judgment hall. Jesus was mighty in weakness. His cross was a throne—His thorns the crown of the universe.

There at the cross, the centurion laid down his sword and shield. There on Golgatha's hill, he laid down his weapons.

Even the centurion could be changed by the power of God. Jesus took that cruel, callous, unfeeling Roman officer and changed him into another man.

A *callous* man became a *converted* man.

A *hard-hearted* man became a *tender, sensitive* man.

He was *changed, transformed, made over again!*

Rather than defending Himself, Jesus loved His enemies. Thus, the hearts of His enemies were broken. Love conquered—love won. The Roman soldier was used to fighting. He knew how to do that well. He was used to defending himself. Yet as he heard the words of his dying Lord—"Father, forgive them," his heart was melted. At the cross, he laid down his weapons.

Can you think of three more seemingly hopeless cases?

1. A stranger from Africa.
2. A thief condemned to death—an inmate on death row.
3. An officer in the Roman army whose callous heart made him eligible for the post of superintendent of executions.

For each of these three men, the deciding factor was the cross.

❑ one carried the cross
❑ one died on a cross
❑ one nailed the Saviour to a cross

The Roman centurion joins the chorus of those inviting you, through the cross, to Christ.

Is your burden heavy? Does the cross you are carrying appear too great? Seize it like Simon, and in so doing, receive life's greatest blessing.

If you are like the Roman centurion, meet God. Lay your weapons down. The battle is over. If you are like the thief, Let Jesus' forgiveness sweep the guilt from your soul. If some burden is crushing out your life, as with Simon, let your cross become your bridge to meet God. This is the Christ of the Scriptures—a Christ who bears burdens, a Christ who alleviates guilt, a Christ who breaks hard hearts and changes men and women. These experiences must be ours!

Like the centurion, I crucify my Saviour and put Him to open shame. At the cross, I lay my weapons down, committing my life to Him. Like the thief, I die with Jesus. ("I am crucified with Christ," see Galatians 2:20.) At the cross, I receive forgiveness. Like Simon, I must take up my cross, daily. I cheerfully bear the burdens Christ allows to come my way.

Will you join me at the cross? Will you look through your tears, guilt, and fear to behold the dying Son of God on the cross? Will you, right now, know and meet Him at the cross? Why not open your heart to His love today?

3

Pilate: Politician Under Pressure

An early spring morning—A.D. 31. Jerusalem, the city of pilgrims' tents, sleeps. It sleeps, that is, except for a band of priests, an unruly crowd, and a prisoner being pushed, coerced, and jostled swiftly through the streets to Pilate's palatial mansion.

Somewhere between five and six in the morning, Pilate is disturbed by knocks on the door. The noisy tumult of the crowd rudely awakens him from a deep sleep. Angrily, he arises. Pilate despises and hates all Jews. He resents their sunrise clamor in the streets of Jerusalem at the very height of the Passover tourist season. But the one thing he doesn't want is trouble from these Jews. His responsibility is to keep peace and protect Roman interests in this far-flung corner of the empire. Tiberius already has doubts about his competency. A riot now could cost him his position.

Tradition tells us that Pilate was a soldier of fortune. Having grown up in army camps, he resolved to make his career in the army. His bravery and dedication to war attracted the attention of Caesar. When asked what reward he wished, Pilate volunteered for the post of Governor of Judea. He well knew that if he failed in this position, his career would end. But if he succeeded in maintaining peace and accomplishing the goals of Rome, there was very little his ambition might not achieve.

Pilate was fiercely loyal to Rome. He desired to advance to the heights of authority, position, and rulership. Such political advancement was his chief goal. To quickly accomplish his dreams, he often acted rashly.

In an attempt to show his loyalty to Rome, Pilate had marched his soldiers into the streets of Jerusalem with their standards flying. Previously, when most Roman governors entered Jerusalem, they had been careful to remove the likeness of the head of the Roman emperor from the top of the flagpoles they carried—in deference to the Jews. The Jews believed that these icons of emperor's heads violated the second commandment that says, "Thou shalt not make unto thee any graven image."

But Pilate had defied all Jewish tradition and marched into Jerusalem with his Roman garrisons—flags flying and the likeness of the emperor's head brazenly displayed. All the might and power of Rome, with its cavalry, chariots, swords, and spears, was brought to bear in Jerusalem against the Jews. For six days, the Jews protested. Pilate threatened them with extermination. At this point, the Jews lay down in the streets with their necks bared, defying Pilate to cut off their heads. This was a great defeat for him. Rumors of this occurrence suggested he was incompetent.

On another occasion, as some Galilean Jews worshiped in the temple at Jerusalem, Pilate ordered his Roman soldiers to enter the temple, massacre them, and mix their blood with the blood of the sacrifices.

This infuriated the Jews, and again a riot in the streets ensued. Pilate, fiercely loyal to Rome, was at a critical place in his career. If anything went wrong in this night trial and the Jews revolted again, Pilate might lose his position. If he could not quell the popular tumult, he might lose the governorship of Judea. His political career might collapse as a deck of cards in the winds. He might be destroyed as a sand castle before the beating waves. A great deal was at stake for Pilate—his honor and prestige were on the line.

False Charges

In the predawn darkness of Jerusalem, Pilate is rudely awakened. Wearily, he drags himself out to meet the Jewish leaders. They immediately bring to him their false accusations against Christ. Now begins to unfold the moving drama of a man who knew better, yet compromised his integrity in order to please the crowd. As this drama progresses, we will compare the wavering and indecision of Pilate to the steadfast faith and commitment of Christ. In Luke 23:1, 2, the Scripture says,

> "The whole multitude of them arose and led Him unto Pilate. They began to accuse Him saying, '[1] We have found this fellow perverting the nation, and [2] forbidding to give tribute to Caesar, saying [3] that he himself is Christ the King.'"

Each charge against Jesus is false. First, Christ was charged with perverting the nation. His accusers claimed He desired to overthrow the government. Second, He was charged with forbidding to pay tribute to Caesar. Third, He was charged with declaring He was a king who wanted to assert authority on an earthly throne.

These charges are amazing, because they are brought forth by Jewish leaders who themselves, in their own hearts, wanted to overthrow the nation, to avoid paying tribute to Caesar, to have their own king. The Jews hated the Romans. They projected on Christ what was in their own hearts. How often frail human beings project upon others what is in their own hearts!

Often what an individual criticizes others about is a problem in his own heart. Our words don't say so much about others as about ourselves. In psychology, this phenomenon is called projection—projecting upon others our own thoughts and motives.

Pilate Believed Jesus to Be Innocent

Pilate saw through the schemes of the Jews. In the innocent, godly bearing of Jesus, Pilate beheld innocence. The governor did not behold rebellion against the government. He didn't behold wickedness. He didn't see a striving, conniving man who wanted to subvert authority.

Pilate asked Jesus a simple question: "Are you king of the Jews?" And in Luke 23:3, Jesus responded directly. Pilate then made his first of three declarations indicating that, as far as he was concerned, there was no fault in Christ. Notice Luke 23:4: "Then said Pilate to the chief priest and to the people, 'I find no fault in this man.'"

What should Pilate have done at this point? If a prisoner is accused and found innocent, what do you do? Obviously, you let him go free. Throughout this story, we see weak, indecisive Pilate manipulated by the crowd. As he declared that there was no fault in Christ, the people were stirred up and began to shout. Infuriated religious leaders, sensing they might lose their victim, urged the crowd on. The scene became one of frenzied intensity. Pilate, sensing that the mob was getting out of control, was afraid they were going to riot.

On the one hand, he knew Jesus was not guilty. He was convinced he ought to release Christ. But he knew that if he did and the crowd rioted—if he were unable to control them, if there were a tumult throughout the city, if during this Passover season Jerusalem exploded into rebellious rioting—he would be removed as governor.

Selfish ambition on the one hand was placed against the eternal value of justice and right on the other. Pilate wavered. He was too indecisive and fearful of the crowd to let Jesus go free. On the other hand, he was convicted that Christ was innocent and was therefore afraid to condemn Him. Pilate weighed out the consequences of the action, not the rightness of the action.

Pilate's First Compromise

Immediately upon hearing that Jesus came from Galilee, Pilate thought of a compromise. During this moving drama, Pilate compromises three times. At each stage, he descends lower in the scale of moral value and comes nearer to giving the crowd what they want.

Pilate attempts to evade responsibility. "I am really not responsible," he insists. This first compromise is recorded in Luke 23:6, 7:

"When Pilate heard of Galilee, he asked whether

the man were Galilean, and as soon as he knew that
he belonged under Herod's jurisdiction he sent him
to Herod who himself was at Jerusalem at the time."

Why send Jesus to Herod? He's innocent. Yet here
Pilate reveals a basic plague spot in his character.
He attempts to evade responsibility. He places all
responsibility squarely upon the shoulders of Herod.
He does not want to bear it himself.

Pilate was greatly troubled by Jesus' godlike bearing. He was convinced that Jesus was more than a
common man. He believed him to be of excellent
character and entirely innocent of the charges
brought against him. He realized a deep plot had
been laid to destroy Jesus, but his inordinate desire
for position hindered him from making the decision
he knew was right.

What people thought of Pilate mattered greatly.
He feared losing power and authority. Out of his own
self interest and his love of honor from the great
men of the earth, he attempted to shift responsibility. "Send Him to Herod," he commanded. "He's not
my responsibility—He's Herod's." Pilate failed to recognize that he was ultimately responsible for his own
actions.

Pilate considered the consequences of the decision rather than its morality. His question was not,
"Is this decision right or wrong?" Rather, his question was, "What results or consequences will I experience if I take this step?"

Compromise often begins with the evasion of responsibility. One of the devil's most subtle falsehoods
is that I am not responsible for my actions. He sug-
gests, "You are not responsible. You choose and act
because of your past or because of your circumstances. But don't worry, God understands."

"I have certain tendencies," he encourages me to

conclude. "I have certain desires bequeathed to me by my parents. I am blunt with people—but that's just the way I am. I was just born that way." Some are led to believe that alcoholism is a disease over which they have no control—that homosexuality is an orientation that cannot change—that anger is simply a personal trait. "That's the way I am. I just have an uncontrollable temper and get hot under the collar."

Environment

In fact, Anna Russell, in the lyrics of a song, captured this relatively modern tendency to avoid taking responsibility:

> *I went to my psychiatrist*
> *To be psycho-analyzed*
> *To find out why I killed the cat*
> *And blackened my wife's eyes.*

> *He put me on a downy couch*
> *To see what he could find,*
> *And this is what he dredged up*
> *From my subconscious mind.*

> *When I was one*
> *My mummy hid my dolly in the trunk,*
> *And so it followed naturally*
> *That I am always drunk.*

> *When I was two*
> *I saw my father kiss the maid one day*
> *That is why I suffer now*
> *Cleptomania.*

> *When I was three*
> *I suffered from ambivalence towards my*
>   *brothers*
> *So it follows naturally*
> *I poisoned all my lovers.*

> _I am so glad that I have learned_
> _The lesson it has taught,_
> _That everything that I did that's wrong_
> _Is someone else's fault._

"Sure, I lose my temper, but that's just the way I am!"

"Sure, I have an appetite problem. Everybody has a problem with something. That's mine."

James placed the responsibility for sin on the shoulders of the one committing it.

> "Every man is tempted when he is drawn away of his own lust and enticed. Then when lust hath conceived, it bringeth forth sin and sin when finished, bringeth forth death." James 1:14, 15.

What is the role of heredity and environment in making us who we are? Others can influence our actions, but they cannot determine our actions. Both Joseph and Daniel faced overwhelming pressure to conform to those around them by compromising their spiritual convictions.

It is easy to shift responsibility for my actions back onto my past, my heredity, or my environment. But that is not the gospel. Revelation 14:7 says, "Fear God and give glory to him, for the hour of his judgment is come." Judgment implies moral responsibility. Judgment implies personal responsibility for my actions. Pilate was responsible for his actions and could not shift that responsibility to Herod.

Any attempt to shift the responsibility for your actions to somebody else is the beginning of compromise. Soon you will excuse open sin. Some declare, "I act the way I act because of somebody else. It's not my responsibility."

The gospel also says that no matter what your

heredity, Jesus Christ has the power to deliver you. In Christ you have forgiveness of sin. Surely your heredity plays a part, but there is something stronger than heredity—the power of the gospel. The gospel is the good news that your sins can be forgiven through Christ and that through Him you can develop new habit patterns in your life. God is big enough to enable you to overcome all inherited and cultivated tendencies toward evil.

Another way some people try to shift responsibility is to blame their environment or circumstances. They offer excuses for their actions.

"My job gives me so much pressure. There is so much cursing and swearing there that I have picked it up."

"My kids put so much pressure on me that I am impatient because of them."

A salesman might reason, "Everyone else is dishonest. In my profession, dishonesty is merely one of the occupational tools we use to succeed."

This attempt to shift responsibility is a part of the very nature of man. It is illustrated in the experience of Billy.

Billy's Attempt to Evade Responsibility

Billy was a four-year-old in his church kindergarten. This little fellow was a terror in his behavior. He pushed the other children, knocked them down, tripped them, and generally kept things upset.

One day the teacher said to him, "Billy, would you like to pray?" This little fighter—this kid who had been pushing others around and knocking them down—prayed a simple little prayer like this: "Lord, please help those little children not to fall down so much."

What a masterful request! In one statement he

had absolved himself of all responsibility for the other children falling down and getting hurt.

We all try to escape responsibility for our actions. Sometimes we blame it on circumstances; other times we are sure someone else made us do what we did. Or we are convinced that we are victims of some cosmic conspiracy. The pressures of life get the blame these days. We try every way we can think of to get around facing up to the situation and admitting the responsibility is ours.

Real change begins with accepting responsibility for our actions. Unless I face up to my responsibility and am willing to declare, "I have failed . . . I did wrong . . . It was my fault"—I will never come to the place of repentance. I will never repent, never see the power of God operate in my life, unless I accept responsibility for my actions.

Don't evade responsibility. It is an essential ingredient for a lifestyle change. Accept it, and then you can go on from there straightening out your life.

My favorite author describes the life-giving power of the cross this way:

> "Those who, through an intelligent understanding of the Scriptures, view the cross aright, those who truly believe in Jesus, have a sure foundation for their faith. They have that faith which works by love and purifies the soul from all its hereditary and cultivated imperfections."—*Testimonies*, vol. 6, p. 238.

The power of living faith is stronger than any weakness I've inherited from my parents or any weakness resulting from repeated falls.

Pilate's attempt to evade responsibility failed. He had to meet the same issue over again. In the development of Christian character, God often confronts us with the same issue again and again. It is God's purpose—as we are repeatedly confronted with the same issues—that we will face them in the power of Christ and come off conquerors.

Pilate's Second Compromise: Indecisiveness and Meeting Sin Halfway

Luke 23:14-16 reveals Pilate's second compromise:

"He said unto them, 'You have brought this man unto me as one who perverts the people, and behold I, having examined him before you, have found no fault in this man, touching those things whereof you accuse him. Nor yet Herod, for I sent you to him, and lo, nothing worthy of death is done unto him. I will therefore chastise him and release him.'"

Why do you whip a man who is innocent? You whip the man if he is guilty, not innocent. To chastise a man in Roman times was a horrible punishment.

Long leather strips imbedded with jagged metal were attached to a solid, short stick. Stripped to his waist with hands tied above his head, the condemned stood as his back was ripped apart. If the torturer wanted, he could wrap the leather around the loins and rip out the bowels. It was possible to wind the leather lash around the stomach of the victim, imbedding the steel barbs into tender flesh and ripping open the stomach.

Pilate desired to show the crowd a little blood. He met sin halfway. He wouldn't crucify Jesus, but he would satisfy the blood-thirsty desires of the crowd. Commenting on this experience in *The Desire of Ages,* Ellen White gives us this penetrating insight:

"Here Pilate showed his weakness. He had declared that Jesus was innocent, yet he was willing for Him to be scourged to pacify His accusers. He would sacrifice principle in order to compromise with the mob. This placed him at a disadvantage. The crowd presumed upon his indecision, and clamored the more for the life of the prisoner. If at the first Pilate had stood firm, refusing to condemn a man whom he found guiltless, he would have broken the fatal chain that was to bind him in remorse and guilt as long as he lived. Had he carried out his convictions of right the Jews would not have presumed to dictate to him. Christ would have been put to death, but the guilt would not have rested upon Pilate. But Pilate had taken step after step in the violation of his conscience. He had excused himself from judging with justice and equity, and he now found himself almost helpless in the hands of the priests and rulers. His wavering and indecision proved his ruin."—Pages 731, 732.

Wavering and indecision proved his ruin. He compromised with sin—he attempted to meet the crowd halfway.

Recently I traveled to Greece. There I learned the fascinating story of one who refused to compromise. He would not meet sin halfway. Discovering the Ten Commandment law, he became convicted, as he studied, that the Sabbath was the seventh day of the week—Saturday. He decided that although, to his knowledge, there were no other Sabbath keepers anywhere in this world, he would be faithful to his conscience and begin keeping the Bible Sabbath.

Since Greece is an Orthodox state, he ultimately was excommunicated from the Greek Orthodox church. In former times this meant that nobody in his community could buy anything from him, and nobody could sell anything to him. His children could not go to school, because all schools were Orthodox schools. He was isolated—imprisoned within his own community. Yet he believed the things he read in the Bible were right.

Three years later, representatives from the Foreign Bible Society visited Greece. As they did, he asked regarding the Bible Sabbath. They gave the usual arguments against it, such as that we are not under the law but under grace—that the day one keeps is not important. Still, they did not dissuade this man.

Through careful questioning, he finally discovered that there were Sabbath keepers in Turkey. Not having their address, he merely wrote to "any Sabbath keepers in Istanbul, Turkey." He continued to press for a response, and over a six-month period, wrote letter after letter.

Finally, after months, a letter was delivered to a small Sabbath keeping church in Istanbul. Contact was set up, and this man learned of the world-wide movement of Seventh-day Adventists and became an Adventist. Ultimately he had to move from his village. God blessed him. His children attended other non-Orthodox schools. He started a little business. God honored him.

Throughout its history, the Christian church has been made strong by those who have conscientiously stood for what they believed to be right without compromising. One violation of conscience leads to another and another and yet another. This was so in the days of Pilate, and it is so today. Pilate did not begin by thinking that he was going to sell out right and truth.

"Pilate at this time had no thought of condemning Jesus [that is, at the beginning of the trial]. He knew the Jews had accused Him through hatred and prejudice. He knew what his duty was. Justice demanded Christ should be immediately released, but Pilate dreaded the ill-will of the people."—*The Desire of Ages,* p. 728.

Pilate Dreaded the Will of the People

Oh, my friends, how terrible! Pilate's fear of the people caused him to crucify Christ. In Luke 23:4, Pilate says, "I find no fault in this man." Verse 14 adds: "I, having examined him before you, have found no fault in this man, touching those things whereof you accuse him." Verse 15: "No, nor yet Herod, for I sent you to him and lo, nothing worthy of death is done unto him." Verse 16: "I would chastise him and release him."

Pilate again clearly states, "I am going to release Him." The crowd goes wild. Again, Pilate attempts to release Jesus. He offers the crowd a choice—Barabbas or Christ. Did you notice that at least four times Pilate tries to release Jesus?

First, Pilate says, "Look, you have a law. Judge Him by your own law." Second, he sends Christ to Herod. Third, he says "I will chastise Him and let Him go." Finally, he says,"You choose—Barabbas or Christ?"

Who was this Barabbas? Barabbas was a rabble-rouser who thought he could take whatever he wanted by extortion or fraud or thievery. Barabbas was a false messiah known for murder and sedition. Barabbas was a hardened criminal—a wretch.

What a choice! Barabbas was a murderer, and Christ was a life-giver. Barabbas was a rebel, and Christ was the Lawgiver. Pilate thought that for sure, the crowd would choose Jesus. When they clamored for Barabbas, Pilate finally washed his hands of the whole thing. Pilate underestimated the crowd. Look at verses 22, 24, and 25. Pilate asks, "What evil has He done?' . . . Pilate gave sentence that it should be as they required. And he released unto them that for sedition and murder was cast into prison whom they had desired, but he delivered Jesus to their will."

The plague spot in Pilate's character was that he played to the crowd. There was one obvious, open, cherished sin in his life—an inordinate desire for position. There was one obvious, cherished ambition. He would pay any price to rule Rome. To do this, he needed popular support. This cherished sin was the door that Satan used to crucify Jesus Christ. Is there some open, known, cherished sin in your life? If there is, Satan will use it to destroy your soul. This is illustrated by an experience that comes out of the troubled country of Haiti.

One Small Nail

A certain Haitian man wanted to sell his house for $2,000. Another man wanted very badly to buy it, but he was poor and couldn't afford the full price. After much bargaining, the owner agreed to sell the house for half the original price, with just one stipulation. He would retain the ownership of one small nail protruding from over the door. After several years, the original owner wanted the house back, but the new owner was unwilling to sell. So the first owner went out and found the carcass of a dead dog and hung it from the single nail he still owned. Soon the house became unlivable. The family was forced to sell the house to the owner of the nail.

If we leave the devil with one small peg in our lives, he will return to hang his rotting garbage on it and make them unfit for Christ's habitation. You must make the choice. Is there some cherished sin in your life? Is there something you are hanging onto that you know is wrong—that you are certain is not in harmony with God's will? One compromise will lead to the next and the next and the next.

Compromise Leads to Ruin

Have you ever wondered how a person—convicted

of sin, moved by the Holy Spirit in the presence of Christ, knowing that Jesus was innocent—could condemn Him to death? It is because he played to the crowd. It is because one compromise led to the next.

But momentarily, let's turn our minds from the compromise of Pilate to the steadfastness of Christ. Christ was unmoved by the taunts of the crowd. In John 19:4, 5, the Scripture says,

> "Pilate therefore went forth again and said unto them, 'Behold I bring him forth to you that you may know that I find no fault in him.' Then came Jesus forth wearing the crown of thorns and the purple robe, and Pilate said unto them, 'Behold the man.'"

Behold the Man

Yes, "Behold the man." Amidst the yelling of the crowd, amidst their screams, as they roar like wild beasts, Jesus stands calmly. "Behold the Man." Behold the crown of thorns jammed upon His head. Behold the red bloody stream that flows like water down His cheeks. Behold His patience amidst abuse. Behold the man.

Behold Him, whipped and flogged. Behold His raw back, torn from the jagged metal barbs imbedded in leather strips. Behold the agony in His eyes. Behold the pain, deeply etched in the lines on His face. Behold the suffering that racks His frame. Behold the man.

Behold the worn, dirty, cast-off robe placed in mocking and ridicule upon His shoulders. Possibly this was one of Pilate's robes. What a sport. Behold the man—the God-man.

Ridiculed, mocked, and laughed at! Behold the reed as a scepter placed in His hand. Behold the soldiers pushing Him. Watch as He is jostled in the crowd. Behold the man.

Watch as clenched fists smash Him in the face. Behold as they pluck out His beard. Behold the man.

The more light you have, the more guilty you become if you don't follow it.

But amidst it all is a divine dignity about His bearing. Amidst it all is a kingly authority that surrounds Him. Amidst it all, Jesus is in control. There is a peace, an inner calm, an authority about this man. Infuriated, Pilate says to Him,

> "Speakest thou not unto me, knowest thou not that I have power to crucify thee and power to release thee? Jesus answered, 'Thou couldst have no power at all against me except it were given thee from above, therefore he that delivered me unto thee hath greater sin.'" John 19:10.

What a truth! Don't miss this. It was Caiaphas, the high priest of the Jewish nation, who delivered Jesus unto Pilate. Although Pilate was guilty, Caiaphas was guiltier still. The more light you have and the more truth God has given, the more guilty you become if you don't follow it. The light of the ages shone upon Caiaphas. All the prophetic truths of the centuries focused upon the coming of the Messiah. He was the fulfillment of Old Testament prophecy, and Caiaphas, the religious leader, missed it.

The light of the ages shines upon us! To compromise, to sell out our Lord, is far more serious for us than if we had never known the truth. (See John 9:40, 41.) Jesus was patient amidst abuse, because He had received strength and power from the Father in the Gethsemane experience and through prayer. He had an inner assurance that in suffering for the sins of man, thousands would live again. He was judged and condemned so that one day man could be free. He knew that one day He would not wear a crown of thorns but a crown of glory. He knew that one day He would not wear a cast-off purple robe from Pilate, but that He would come as King of kings and Lord of lords, clothed with the righteousness that was His as God.

Again, Behold the Man

In John 19:5, Pilate says, "Behold the man." Here he spoke a truth. Jesus was the God-man. God suffering. God dying. God tabernacling in human flesh. It was the God-man who suffered abuse. It was the God-man who suffered ridicule. It was the God-man who suffered mockery. Yet Pilate spoke the truth in John 19:14 as well! "And it was the preparation of the Passover about the sixth hour, and he said unto the Jews, 'Behold your king.'"

Here Pilate spoke a truth—a truth so significant that even he did not understand it. Behold your King. Even in the midst of the mockery, ridicule, horror, pain, and suffering of it all, Jesus was King. Through the sorrow and agony, clothed in soiled garments, with blood-stained brow and a lacerated back, He was still King. His whole being gave evidence of kingly authority. He stood unmoved by the fury of the waves which beat about Him.

It was as if the heavy surges of wrath, rising higher and higher like the waves of the boisterous ocean, broke about Him but did not touch Him. He stood silent amidst the rebuke, and His silence was eloquent.

It was as if a light shone from the inner man and radiated throughout Him. He was King. As He stood silently, He prayed for Pilate. He asked His heavenly Father to impress Pilate's mind. In answer to His prayer, an angel was sent to Pilate's wife, who revealed to her in a dream that Jesus was the divine Son of God. She saw that Christ was the fulfillment of prophecies. She saw that He was to die for the sins of men. She saw that through His death, forgiveness could be given to all mankind. She saw that this Christ would come again as King of kings and Lord of lords and as Judge of all the earth.

Quickly, she wrote a note to her husband encouraging him to release Jesus. Pilate's wife saw the judgment scene. She beheld her husband condemned at the judgment bar of God. She watched in horror as Jesus, King of kings and Lord of lords, returned in glory. Still, Pilate—wishing to please the crowd—did not have the moral courage to release Jesus. Placing his hands in the water basin and washing them, he said, "I shall have nothing to do with this just man." Pilate walked away from Jesus. In his final moment of conviction, his golden opportunity passed. Pride and ambition and love of position, honor, and power kept him from making the decision he knew he ought to make. Yet in his compromise, he lost all that he desired.

Pilate's Ultimate Fate

History tells us that after several stupid acts of unnecessary cruelty inflicted by Pilate upon the Jews, the Samaritans complained to Rome. Pilate was summoned, stripped of his honors, and relieved of his position. Exiled and broken, he lost his wealth and power. His position was taken and another appointed in his place. Humiliated, in despair, and drunken, he committed suicide.

In Pilate, we see one who watched God executed. He placed against eternal truth and eternal righteousness the ambitions of the passing moment. Pilate put his friendship with Caesar uppermost in his life and crucified the Son of God. The future, he squandered for the here and now. Its transient honors, its fading glories, its transitory privileges, he bought with the denial of truth, flinging aside justice with cruelty and useless mockery of right. In making this choice, he squandered everything.

One day, as Christ streams down the corridors of time and the heavens are illuminated with the glory of the coming of God, each actor in the drama of salvation will see exactly the part he or she has played. One day, the panorama of the crucifixion will be played on the great TV screen of the sky. Each person will see his or her part in that drama (see Philippians 2:9-11).

> "The awful spectacle appears just as it was. Satan, his angels, and his subjects have no power to turn from the picture of their own work. Each actor recalls the part which he performed. Herod who slew the innocent children of Bethlehem that he might destroy the King of Israel, the base Herodius upon whose guilty soul rests the blood of John the Baptist. The weak time-serving Pilate. All behold the enormity of their guilt."—*The Great Controversy*, p. 667.

It did not have to end that way for Pilate. He could have gone down in history as the Roman ruler who had the courage to release Christ. His influence could have blessed thousands of others. His name could have been associated with steadfastness and loyalty and righteousness, as were those of Daniel and Joseph and Paul. But he played to the crowd. He compromised. Pilate's judgment hall is set up before us again. And again the question Pilate asked comes ringing home to our hearts: "What then will you do with this Christ?"

Pilate's decision is your decision and mine. The poet Albert B. Simpson penned that decision in these words:

> *Jesus is standing in Pilate's hall,*
> *Friendless, forsaken, betrayed by all,*

Hearken what meaneth the sudden call,
What will you do with Jesus?

What will you do with Jesus?
Neutral you cannot be.
Some day you will be asking,
What will He do with me?

4

Gethsemane: Crisis in the Garden

For over three thousand years, Israel has been the center of conflict. Although little more than 120 miles long from north to south, this finger-like projection of land has played a vital part in shaping the history and destiny of the world. As a land bridge between three continents—Africa, Asia, and Europe—it is a significant, strategic point on the eastern end of the Mediterranean Sea.

Israel is also the center of three great religions of the world—Judaism, Islam, and Christianity. Jerusalem, its capital, is the focal point for each of these religions. In the magnificent Dome of the Rock, the followers of Mohammed believe their faith was born.

According to Islamic tradition, Abraham was commanded by God to offer up Ishmael on this very spot. It was from the Dome of the Rock that Muslims believe Mohammed ascended to heaven. The Dome of the Rock is the world's second-most holy place for Muslims. The birthplace of Mohammed—Mecca—is, of course, their most sacred spot.

Jews look to Jerusalem—where their temple was built (a thousand years before Christ) at the time of David and Solomon—as the center of Judaism. Thousands of Jews visit the Wailing Wall to pray for the coming of their messianic King and conqueror. The Jews see in the Wailing Wall the magnificent glory of a bygone age. They still look for a Messiah who will come and deliver them from the bondage of their enemies and usher in wealth and splendor.

Christians, of course, look to Israel as intimately tied to the redemption of man. Jesus was born in Bethlehem, grew up in Nazareth, ministered in Galilee and Judea, was tried and crucified in Jerusalem, and ascended from the Mount of Olives. Christians think of Bethlehem as Christ's birthplace, Nazareth as His hometown, and Palestine as the land of His ministry. Jerusalem is the city He died in—the Garden Tomb the place of His resurrection.

Israel is Christ's land. Beyond the political and social turmoil, over two thousand years ago a battle, waged for the destiny of the human race. The garden of Gethsemane in the heart of Jerusalem was the center, the focal point, the heart, of this eternal conflict.

The battle for the dominion of the world began in a garden—and it was settled in a garden. In a garden called Eden, Satan, in the form of a serpent, deceived our first parents. In a garden, they lost the dominion of the earth. In a garden called Gethsemane, Christ met with Satan in conflict. In a garden, He made the decisive choice to go to the cross so that human beings once again could live in the earth made new! From a tree in the garden, Satan brought his most subtle temptations to our first parents. The destiny of the world hung in the balance. The battle was waged—and lost. Once again in a garden, beneath olive trees, the destiny of the world hung in the balance. The tempter again came with all of his subtle deceptions. The battle was waged, and, thank God, this time in the garden, it was won!

Gethsemane: Jesus' Private Place of Prayer

In Jerusalem there were no gardens of any size. A city set atop a hill, as Jerusalem was, had no room for gardens. Every inch was valued for building. Wealthy citizens had private gardens on the slopes of the Mount of Olives. Gethsemane means an "olive vat" or "olive press." No doubt it was a small olive grove to which Jesus had the right of entry.

It is interesting to note the many nameless friends who rallied around Jesus in His last days: The man who loaned Him the donkey on which He rode into Jerusalem . . . the man who allowed Him use of the upper room where the last supper was eaten . . . the man who gave Him permission to use the garden. Amid the hatred and ridicule and mockery of the crowds were oases of love.

The Gospels of Matthew and Mark identify the garden as Gethsemane. The Gospel of Luke doesn't designate the place by name but merely says, "When He was at the place." The Gospel of John accounts for Judas' knowledge of "the place" from its being a frequent resort of the Saviour. Jesus often came to this spot. Situated a little more than half a mile from the city of Jerusalem and a short distance from the brook Kidron on the western slope of the Mount of

Olives, it was an ideal quiet spot for prayer. Jesus had His private, sacred place of prayer where He could fellowship with the Father.

Just after the last supper, in company with His disciples, the Saviour slowly made His way to this—one of His favorite spots—Gethsemane. The Passover moon was broad and full as it shone from a cloudless sky. Jerusalem, a city of pilgrims assembled to celebrate the Passover, was hushed, sleeping in silence. As Jesus and His disciples walked from the site of the upper room down the Kidron Valley, across the brook Cherith, and up the slopes of the Mount of Olives, Jesus earnestly discussed His coming fate with them. As He neared Gethsemane, He became strangely silent. He had often visited this spot for meditation and prayer, but never with a heart so full of sorrow as on this—the night of His last agony.

In the garden today are eight olive trees whose age is lost in antiquity. Probably they are not the same trees under which Jesus prayed. The historian Josephus relates that Titus cut down all the trees within Jerusalem in A.D. 70 when he destroyed the city. Though some botanists claim that the trees may be more than two thousand years old, this seems highly unlikely. But if in fact these trees escaped destruction, they are indeed the very contemporaries of Christ.

Pliny makes an interesting statement. He says that "the olive tree does not die." Though Titus may have cut them to the ground, their roots undoubtedly sprang up to produce new trees which bore still more fruit. Jesus was cut down like the olive tree. His blood poured out like the oil of the olive. He was crushed like the olive. He died—only to bear fruit again. His death was as the seed for a thousand—yea, ten thousand times ten thousand—to live.

Jesus received power in the secret place of prayer to place His will on God's side. His statement, "The spirit is willing, but the flesh is weak," spoken to the sleeping disciples, simply means that without a personal relationship with God through prayer, we may desire to do right, but in the flesh have no power or strength to carry out the decision.

Jesus suffered in Gethsemane: Why?

Mark 14:32 records the scene this way:

> "And they came to a place which was named Gethsemane. And he said to His disciples. 'Sit you here while I shall pray.' And he taketh with him Peter, James and John and began to be sore amazed and to be very heavy. And he said unto them, 'My soul is exceeding sorrowful unto death, tarry you here and watch.'"

The Phillips translation of Mark 14:32 says that Jesus was "horror stricken and desperately depressed." The New English Bible says that "horror and dismay came over Him." The Living Bible says: "My soul is crushed by sorrow to the point of death, filled with horror and the deepest distress." Why was Jesus so amazed, horror stricken, and distressed?

Gethsemane was the center of a cosmic conflict—the focus of a titanic struggle between good and evil. In the garden, Jesus experienced the heat of severe battle between the forces of hell and the forces of heaven.

Fritz Rienecker and Leon Rodgers, in their linguistic key to the New Testament, give us these additional details about the meaning of the words *amazed* and *distressed*: "Someone in the grip of a shuddering horror, in the face of a dreadful prospect before him." The poet captures the magnitude and significance of what was taking place in Gethsemane with these words:

Gethsemane

"Wouldst thou learn the depths of sin,
All its bitterness and pain;
What it cost thy God to win
Sinners to Himself again?
Come, poor sinner, come with me;
Visit sad Gethsemane."

Jesus certainly faced dreadful prospects. The full burden of sin came crashing down upon Him in Gethsemane. Isaiah 53:4 says: "Surely he hath borne our griefs and carried our sorrows, yet we did esteem him stricken, smitten of God, and afflicted."

Isaiah 63:8 adds: "In all their affliction he was afflicted."

2 Corinthians 5:21 says: "He who knew no sin became sin for us."

The *corporate, combined, accumulated* guilt of the ages rested upon Christ (see also Galatians 3:13). In Gethsemane, Jesus was enveloped by the darkness of the evil one. The weight of the world's sin pressed upon Him. The condemnation that sin brings filled his heart with "horrors." The prophet Isaiah declares (Isaiah 59:2) that "Your iniquities have separated you from God." Not only does sin separate man from God—it separated Jesus from God.

What does sin do to us? It separates us from God. What did sin do to Jesus as our sin bearer? It separated Him from God.

Separated From the Father

Ellen White puts it this way in the book *The Desire of Ages:*

"Christ was standing in a different attitude from that in which He had ever stood before. . . . As the substitute and surety for sinful man Christ was suffering under divine justice. He saw what justice meant. Hitherto He had been as an intercessor for others. Now He longed to have an intercessor for Himself. As Christ felt His unity with the Father broken up He feared that in His human nature He would be unable to endure the coming conflict with the powers of darkness."—page 686.

Let's consider Christ's difficult choice in those titanic struggles. He could take the risk of redeeming man at the expense of destroying Himself—without any certain knowledge they would respond—or He could save Himself.

Describing the intense battle waged by the forces of hell, Luke gives us this insight: "This is your hour and the power of darkness." Luke 22:53.

The powers of darkness engulfed Christ. According to *The Desire of Ages:*

> "Satan told Him that if He became the surety for a sinful world the separation would be eternal. He would be identified with Satan's kingdom and would never more be one with God. How hopeless it appeared for Christ. In its hardest features Satan pressed the battle upon the Redeemer of mankind."—page 687.

Notice how this statement continues. Observe particularly the viciousness with which Satan attacked Christ:

> "He [Satan] asserted the people who claim to be above all others in spiritual advantages would reject Him, and seek to destroy Him. His own people, the Jews, would turn their backs on Him. One of His own disciples who listened to His instruction day by day, Judas, would betray Him. One of His most zealous followers, Peter, would deny Him. All would forsake Him."—page 688.

No wonder Christ was filled with such darkness and loneliness. No wonder He was stunned with horror and oppressed. It appeared to Him that He would be separated eternally from the Father and that His sacrifice would be unappreciated even by His closest followers. It was this inner agony that proved far more intense than any physical suffering .

Certainly Jesus was well aware of the physical horrors of crucifixion. At thirty-three years of age and in the prime of life, obviously He did not want to die. Yet was it the prospect of physical death that caused Jesus such intense agony of mind?

Was Jesus' Attitude in Facing Death Different Than That of the Martyrs?

Consider the martyrs. Many courageously faced death in its most ghastly forms. Some endured cruel tortures without complaint . . . some were torn apart by wild beasts . . . some were left to look at the approaching tide as it drew nearer and still nearer . . . some were crucified with their head downward . . . some were burned at the stake . . . some were sawn in half.

Many of different ranks and in different ages have submitted to the cruelest tortures, undaunted and undismayed. Did the servant surpass his Master in suffering? Did the disciple surpass his Lord in agony? Certainly the suffering of Jesus Christ was far different than the suffering of the martyrs. They were sustained by the presence of God. They felt and experienced the power of God, but Jesus, dying as a sin-bearer, bore the weight of the sins of the world. Jesus longed for two things at Gethsemane:

1. He longed for human fellowship—for the amazing power of human love.

2. He longed for divine fellowship—He craved the assurance of His Father's love and care. He yearned for a sense of the divine sustaining presence.

The Bitter Cup

At creation, God Himself stated a universal truth in Genesis 2:18: "It is not good that man should be alone." In a time of suffering, we want somebody with us. In a time of trouble, we want somebody near. Sometimes we don't want them to do or say anything—we just want them to be there. Notice Jesus' prayer in Mark 14:35: "And he went forward a little and fell on the ground and prayed that if it were possible the hour might pass from him."

What was Jesus praying? He was saying, "Father, if it is possible, save the human race in some other way. If it is possible to save the world without this suffering, agony, horror, and death—if it is possible to save them without this intense struggle, this loneliness, this isolation—if it is possible to save man without this terrible, painful separation—if it is possible, Father, let this cup pass from me!"

Where Mark's Gospel declares, "let this hour pass," Matthew words it a little differently (compare Mark 14:35 to Matthew 26:39). Matthew says, "He went a little further and fell on his face and prayed, saying, 'Oh my Father, if it is possible let this cup pass from me. Nevertheless not as I will but as thou wilt.'"

The "cup" in Scripture is a common expression for suffering. Jesus prayed, let this cup—this cup of bitterness, this cup of sorrow, this cup of agony, this cup of horror, this cup of loneliness and isolation, this cup of darkness—let this cup pass from me.

Every human being, sometime in life, is handed the cup. You can take one of three attitudes toward the cup. You can resent the cup and become bitter that it has been handed to you. You can run from the cup and attempt to evade it. Or you can receive the cup with perfect trust in the care of your loving heavenly Father.

Jesus did not fully understand why He had to drink such a bitter cup. He only knew that beyond a doubt it was the will of God. Jesus had to make a great venture of faith to accept, as we often do, the cup of suffering He could not understand. Nobody wants to die, and at thirty-three, in the garden, Jesus was quite sure that death lay ahead of Him. Here Jesus experienced a supreme struggle to submit His will to the will of God.

This is the struggle of every Christian. The Christian life is not centered on feelings or emotions but on the will. This is not to say that a Christian has no feeling or emotions—he or she certainly does. But it is to say that the essence of the Christian life is responding to the claims of Christ, the promptings of the Holy Spirit, and the love of God, by placing the will on the side of right. The will is the governing power in the nature of man—the power of decision or of choice.

Jesus' temptation in Gethsemane was focused on whether He would yield to His personal feelings and emotions or surrender in perfect trust to the revealed will of God.

The salvation of the world swayed in the balance. Here Jesus learned the lesson that all some day must learn—how to accept what we cannot understand. Things happen to each of us that we don't understand. Faith is tried to the limits. The early church father Tertullian said, "No one who has not been tempted can enter the kingdom of heaven." Every man or woman has a private Gethsemane in which he or she must learn to say, "Thy will be done."

In Mark 14:36 is a wonderful expression indicating Jesus' trust in this time of sorrow: "And he said, 'Abba, Father, all things are possible unto thee. Take away this cup from me, nevertheless not as I will but as thou wilt.'"

Jesus' use of this word—*abba*—is unparalleled in all Jewish literature. *Abba* is the word a young child used to address his father—an everyday family word, a word that indicates childlike, trustful obedience.

Even when He did not understand, He called the Father "Daddy." Confronted with the cross, faced with darkness and despair, tempted to mistrust, He called His Father "Daddy." What words of supreme trust!

In the days of the counter-reformation in England, Richard Cameron, that great man of faith and courage, was martyred by the church-state government official, Murray.

Cameron's head and hands were cut off and brought to his father, who was in prison for the same crime in Scotland. As the boy's mangled, bloody arms and head were brought to his father for the express purpose of giving him added grief, the official asked, "Are these the arms and head of your son, Richard? Do you recognize them?"

With tears streaming down his cheeks, the father gently reached out and embraced the arms and head of his son. His lips quivered. Gently, he spoke, "I know them. I know them. They are my son's—my own dear son's. But it is the Lord who grants me mercy all the days of my life. Good is the will of the Lord, who can not wrong me or mine."

Even the work of the enemy in destroying his son could not shake the faith of the elder Cameron in his God. A deep sense that a loving heavenly Father cannot and will not do one evil to me but will constantly sustain me, makes all the difference. It provides a deep inner peace.

If we call God our Father, everything in life becomes bearable. Time and again, we will not understand, but we know the Father's hand will never cause His children needless pain or a needless tear. Trials descend, heartaches come, difficulties confront us, yet Jesus' love is constant. In the midst of suffering and sorrow, Jesus cried out, "Father, Father, Thy will be done." That is not to say that all of the sickness and sorrow and anxiety in life is good, but it is to say that in spite of that sickness, suffering, sorrow, and heartache, God is good.

Life may not be fair, but God is fair. When we don't understand—as Jesus didn't understand—we can trust, and we can say, "God, in the midst of this situation, Thy will be done." How we say it makes all the difference. The expression, "Not my will but your will" can be uttered in varying ways.

Four Ways to Say "Thy Will Be Done"

First, I can say it in hopeless submission—as one who is in the grip of a power so overpowering that it seems useless to fight. In other words, I can't do anything about it; therefore I can only hopelessly submit to the circumstances. For example, in the grip of illness—dying of cancer in a hospital—I can say, "Thy will be done," and say it in hopeless resignation.

Second, I can say it as one who has been battered into submission. The pressures of life have become too great. I have been battered, knocked down. This is the call of one who is defeated because the enemy is too powerful—like a defeated army general who says, "Here's my sword—your will be done." I can say it with hopeless resignation, or I can say it as one who has been battered into submission.

Third, I can say it as one who is utterly frustrated, who sees his dreams broken and smashed so they will never come true. The words may be of regret or of bitter anger—anger made all the more bitter because I can't do anything about what is causing it.

Or I can say it with the confidence of perfect trust. This is how Jesus said it. He was speaking to one who was His Father—to one who held His hand, one who had His everlasting arms beneath. He was submitting to a love that would not let Him go.

Learning to Trust

When I was a boy, my grandfather raised canaries, and I remember going up into the attic of 9 Raymond Place, Norwich, Connecticut, and watching as my grandfather whistled to the canaries. I watched in amazement as he took one canary and put it in a cage alone, then covered the cage so the bird was in total darkness. Then he began to whistle, and as he whistled, the canary heard the voice of its master. Surprisingly enough, the canary picked up the whistle or tune. Soon, in the darkness alone, hearing the tune, the canary began to sing it. The song learned in the darkness, the bird sings forever after.

God is teaching you and me to trust, as He taught Jesus to trust. One of the greatest lessons of life is to learn to trust when we cannot understand—to learn to trust when it seems dark, when the journey seems long and the way seems hard, when there is no way around or over or through the mountain.

Trust does not mean that I understand what is happening to me. Trust does not mean that what is happening to me is fair and just. Trust does not mean that the experiences I am going through are right. Trust does not mean that they are always God's primary purpose for my life. But trust does mean that I understand that God loves me, that He cares for me, and that through this experience He is going to bring me out triumphant.

The poet puts it this way:

> *"God, thou art love, I will build my faith on that,*
> *I know thou who hast kept my path*
> *And made light for me in the darkness,*
> *Tempering sorrows so that they reached me like*
> *   solemn joy.*
> *It were too strange that I should doubt thy love."*
> —Francis Xavier

Jesus spoke like that, and we can speak like that. We can look up, and in perfect trust and submission say, "God, Thy will be done." As Jesus prayed and the disciples slept, the battle intensified.

The Battle Intensifies

As Jesus prayed, an angel descended to strengthen Him. Notice Luke 22:44: "And being in agony he prayed more earnestly and His sweat was as it were great drops of blood falling to the ground."

Medical literature indicates that it is possible, under the stress of excessive terror or extreme exhaustion, for a man to sweat drops of blood. In fact, Voltaire, the French skeptic, in his essay on the civil wars of France, described a scene in which a man sweat blood.

King Charles IX, soon after the St. Bartholomew's massacre—that bloodbath in which thousands were massacred—was attacked by a strange malady against which the art and skill of physicians was unavailing. His blood oozed out, for-cing its way through the pores of his skin. As Voltaire described it, he said this was the result of excessive fear—of violent struggle within and the divine vengeance of God against sin.

Jesus, in the garden of Gethsemane, experienced this violent struggle within. The judgment bar of God was set up and, bearing the sins of the world, He sweat, as it were, great drops of blood. But when the struggle was the most intense and fierce, Jesus continued praying, and Luke 22:43 says, "And there appeared an angel unto him from heaven, strengthening him."

The hymn says:

> *"Just when I need Him, Jesus is near,*
> *Just when I falter,*
> *Just when I fear,*
> *Just when I need Him most."*

Strengthened by the Angel

It is interesting to observe that the angel came only after Christ made the decision to do the Father's will.

When it appeared that the load of sin was too great for Christ—when it appeared He would die fainting beneath the load, overwhelmed by sin—an angel from heaven appeared to strengthen Him. This angel did not come to take the cup from His hand, to deliver Him from suffering and anxiety, to take the trial away from Him. The angel came to strengthen Him, to empower Him, to give Him courage and the assurance of His Father's presence.

As Jesus rose from prayer, He arose strengthened to face the conflict, empowered to face the mob, and filled with new courage to face the farce of the trial, betrayal, and Calvary's hill. What a contrast between Jesus and the disciples. Luke 22:45 says:

> "And when he rose up from prayer and was come to his disciples, he found them sleeping. He said to them, 'Why sleep you, rise up and pray lest you enter into temptation.' And while he yet spake, behold

a multitude and he that was called Judas, one of the twelve, went before them and drew near unto Jesus to kiss Him."

A praying Redeemer and sleeping disciples. What a contrast! In the struggle and conflict, He prayed. In the struggle and conflict, they slept. Jesus sensed that alone, He had no strength to meet the adversary. Self-confidently, they felt they had strength to meet the tempter.

Jesus drew strength from His Father to meet the trials and difficulties that lay ahead. They slept. Lethargically and sluggishly, they slept. It was not a deep sleep. He had attempted to warn them that the mob was coming, but they failed to recognize the overwhelming temptations Satan had in store for them.

We may desire to do right, but without supernatural power derived from a relationship with God in prayer, we cannot accomplish it. All our desires and promises are like ropes of sand. If there is little prayer, our devotional life is weak, and our human will constantly fights for supremacy.

God calls us to something deeper than an external attraction to biblical doctrines and a cultural lifestyle. He invites us to a devotional experience wherein we—in our own Gethsemane—settle the issue of surrendering our will.

Peter's Experience

Peter was self-confident. He saw little need for intense prayer. And Peter denied his Lord. "I don't know Him!" exclaimed Peter, as he cursed and swore. Jesus marched to the cross, and Peter ran into the shadows, denying his Lord, .

Temptation is coming for you and for me, and the greatest conflict of the ages will soon break upon us. Again, the mob will come. Again, God's people will face trial, and again some of them will be subject to death.

Many today are sleeping. Their prayers are spasmodic, careless, lethargic—their spiritual experience weak. Few know how to pray through problems as Jesus prayed them through in Gethsemane. The storm is coming, relentless in its fury. Yet, just as the angel came to strengthen Christ in His experience of prayer, God desires to send heavenly angels to strengthen you and me. All the forces of heaven are available for God's children, and the weakest saint in Christ is strong enough to meet all the hosts of hell and the adversary, the devil.

Right now, Jesus is speaking to your heart. When you don't understand the trials and difficulties of life, He invites you to trust. When the heartaches and sorrows of life overwhelm you, He invites you to trust. If you are lonely and alone, feeling overpowered by the temptations of Satan, He invites you to look to Him—and the same God who sent strength to Jesus will send it to you. The same God who gave Him courage to face the trial will give you courage to face your trial. When you are spiritually lethargic and drowsy, He invites you to hang on, and in prayer and faith, He will revive your soul.

A Surrender Without Reservations

On December 8, 1934, Chinese bandits murdered two Presbyterian missionaries, John and Betty Stam, and burned their home to the ground. Some days after the tragedy, friends found among the charred ruins the flyleaf of Mrs. Stam's Bible. On it were written these touching words of dedication:

> "Lord, I give up my purpose and plans, all my desires, hopes, and ambitions, and accept Thy will for my life. I give myself, my life, my all utterly to Thee to be Thine forever. I hand over to Thy keeping all

my friendships, my love. All the people whom I love are to take second place in my heart. Fill me and seal me with Thy Holy Spirit. Work out Thy whole life in my life at any cost now and forever. For me to live is Christ, and to die is gain."

Why not make that same surrender to His will right now as well!

5

Love Bathed in Agony

Braun was born of English parents. He was just a little boy, nine or ten years old. His parents were wealthy and lived in a British village not far from London—a village with quaint country lanes and cobblestone streets. They were not Christians—they were agnostics.

But Braun's parents felt that at least once in his life, he needed to go to church. They dressed him up in his little black suit and black bow tie and asked the governess to take him to church. Since this was a little over a hundred years ago, a horse-drawn carriage carried the boy to church for the very first time.

It was one of those quaint little country churches.

The preacher talked about a man nailed to a wooden cross. He described the nails driven through the man's hands, the crown of thorns jammed upon His head, the blood that ran down His face, and the spear that ripped apart His side. He described the agony in His eyes and the sorrow in His voice when He prayed, "Father, forgive them, for they don't know what they are doing."

He described the Saviour's overwhelming despair when He cried, "My God, My God, why have You forsaken me?" And he recalled Jesus' faith, when in commitment He said, "Father, into Thy hands I commit my Spirit."

Braun was moved by it all. Wouldn't somebody do something? Wouldn't the congregation that day rise up in one accord and take the man down from the cross? Soon little Braun, halfway through the sermon, was crying. As he looked around in astonished surprise, he saw the old deacon in the back of the church, sleeping. He saw two teenagers talking, and he noticed others pointing to a hat or a dress—and one man seemed to be reading the newspaper hidden underneath his Bible as the preacher talked about the cross.

"What is the matter with these people, Nanny?" Braun asked. "Why doesn't somebody do something about that man on the cross?"

Braun's nanny nervously replied, "Braun, Braun, be quiet," as she tapped him on the shoulder. "It is just a story. Don't let it trouble you. Just listen quietly. You will soon forget about this old story when we go home."

Is the cross just a story for you? Is the cross something you sometimes sing about? Something you occasionally mention in prayer? Something you hear glibly mentioned in sermons? Or has the cross reached down into your life and fundamentally changed you at the core?

What difference does the cross make in your marriage? What difference does the cross make in the relationship you have with your husband, wife, or children? What difference does the cross make when you have differences of opinion with others? What difference does the cross make in your business dealings? What difference does the cross make in your despair and discouragement? What difference does the cross make to a woman who has just been diagnosed with breast cancer and told that she has six months to live? What difference does the cross make then?

I am not as interested in how some people understand the cross theologically as I am in how the cross affects my life. How does it make me a new man? How does it transform my relationships with my children and my wife and other people around me? What difference does the cross make to a man struggling with guilt and fear and worry and perplexity and despair? What difference does the cross make in the nitty-gritty of life where we live it in the twentieth century? I think it makes a difference—a significant difference.

The cross makes a difference because of four revelations it makes:

1. The cross reveals the magnitude of God's forgiveness.

The apostle Paul states it clearly in Romans 5:8, 9:

> "But God commendeth his love toward us, in that, while we were yet sinners, Christ died for us. Much more then, being justified by his blood, we shall be saved from wrath through him."

Let's focus now on verse 10: "For if, when we were enemies, we were reconciled to God by the death of his Son, much more, being reconciled, we shall be saved by his life."

We were His enemies—and He is our Friend. God is not the enemy of His enemies. We deserve death; He gives us life. We deserve condemnation; He acquits us. We deserve a crown of thorns; He gives us the crown of glory. We deserve to be hung up on a tree, but He is nailed there. We deserve the cross; He gives us the throne.

Come with me to Pilate's judgment hall and see there a man stripped to His waist, His hands tied above His head. Behold as strong-armed Roman soldiers approach Him with their leather whips in which bits of bone and steel are imbedded. Listen to the whips snap and watch as sharp, jagged metal edges dig into human flesh. Behold as the executioner rips hunks of flesh out of His back—and watch the blood run like water. He takes our whipping; He suffers the pain of death so that we do not have to experience its agony.

Come with me next up a hill called Calvary to a place called Golgotha and watch as Jesus stumbles three times beneath the load. Watch as His arms are stretched out on a cross. Behold as the Roman soldiers drive crude, jagged nails through His hands. Listen to the thud of the cross into the hole dug for it. Listen to His words, "Father, forgive them, for they don't know what they are doing."

Judas betrayed Him. Peter denied Him. The Jews forsook Him. The cross is unjust. You do not nail a man to the cross who touched the eyes of the blind and they immediately opened . . . a man who touched the ears of the deaf and they were unstopped . . . a man who touched withered arms and legs and they instantly came to life. You don't nail a man to the cross who raised the dead. The cross is unfair; the cross is unjust. But Jesus says, "Father, forgive them, for they don't know what they are doing."

Coming to the cross, I receive forgiveness so that I can forgive. I can forgive my wife, my children, and my neighbors when they treat me unjustly. At the cross, I find Christ's forgiveness, so I can become forgiving. At the cross, I find mercy, so I can become merciful. At the cross, I hear the echo of the words of Paul: "Be you kind one to another, tender-hearted and forgiving one another, even as God, for Christ's sake, has forgiven you." Ephesians 4:32.

Has somebody wronged you? Is there bitterness in your heart toward someone? Do you look back over your childhood, see the way your parents raised you, and think, "They just didn't give me the child-hood I wanted. It is not fair that my father was an alcoholic. It is not fair that Mom left Dad for another man."

Are you carrying around some bitterness or anger or resentment? At the cross, you can find a Christ who forgives you, and you can have the forgiveness to forgive them.

Mister, are you upset with something your wife said to you this morning? Even as you read these words, are you are filled with resentment? At the cross, Jesus forgave you; therefore you can forgive her. Are you upset with some church member who was unjust or unfair in doing business with you? Have you ever angrily said to yourself, "If that is the way they treat me, I want nothing to do with the church"? Jesus forgave those who wronged Him. They nailed Him to the cross. And the essence of Christianity is the ability to forgive people who have wronged you.

Corrie ten Boom was taken captive by the Ger-mans and brought to Ravensbruck Prison Camp. I have often visited Dachau and Auschwitz, having conducted evangelistic meetings in Poland and Germany. Visiting these prison camps is a life-changing experience. They are horrible places of death.

From all over Europe, Nazi officers gathered these refugees. They were taken by train to what they were told was to be a retreat center away from the ravages and horrors of war. Between 1939 and 1944, these trains transported thousands to the factories of death. As the prisoners arrived, they were greeted with bands playing lively, joyful songs of happiness. Their initial feelings were of relief, believing they had been delivered from the ravages of war. They understood that they were being relocated and fully expected that soon after the war was over, they would return to their homes. But once they got off the trains, they learned all too quickly that they had entered a place of death. Some would be gassed immediately; others within a month. But no one would live more than six months. In Auschwitz, for example, the furnaces burned for six consecutive years, twenty-four hours a day. Ultimately, over six million were murdered.

When Corrie ten Boom was mistakenly released from the prison camp, she was one of the few who got out alive. She was so moved by her experiences that she set up a home in Holland for those who had been prisoners of the German Gestapo. She said that the difference between those who suffered mental breakdowns and those who recovered after the horrors they experienced was their ability to forgive. Those who could not forgive—who bore bitterness and resentment—were often mentally unbalanced for the rest of their lives. Corrie took the message of God's forgiveness and brought God's love to that bombed-out land of Germany in 1945 and 1946.

One night she spoke in Munich. After eloquently describing God's forgiveness to hundreds of eager listeners, she noticed one man in the crowd. After the service, he approached her. He was a stocky man, five feet and ten inches, with deeply set eyes and a square face.

She would never forget him. He had been one of the most cruel guards in Ravensbruck. She remembered when her sister, Betsie, had passed before him and he had reached up and pulled Betsie's blouse off to embarrass her. She remembered when this very man now approaching her in Munich had reached out with his fist and hit Betsie in the face. She remembered Betsie's screams of agony, and she remembered that as Betsie fell, this Gestapo sergeant had taken his leather boot and purposely crushed Betsie's ribs. She remembered the sound of the bones cracking and the pain Betsie suffered—and she remembered Betsie withering down to ninety pounds and dying in that prison camp.

Now, after the war, this man stood before Corrie. He reached out his hand and asked, "Corrie, would you forgive me?" And Corrie said, "I wanted to spit in his face. I wanted to reach out and slap him across the face. Every emotion in me cried out for revenge. But I said to myself, 'No, I cannot.' I knew that unless I forgave him, every ounce of love in me would dry up. I knew that bitterness and resentment and unwillingness to forgive would eat out my spiritual heart."

Forgiveness is a choice to release another from your condemnation because Christ has released you from His condemnation. It is treating them as if they had always loved you.

Contrary to conflicting feelings within, Corrie reached out, grasped the man's hand, and sobbed out, "Brother, I forgive you." She recalled, "When I reached out my hand, I reached out against all the inclinations within me. When I said those words, 'Brother, I forgive you,' immediately a new peace flooded through my life."

Is there somebody you need to tell that you forgive them? Is there somebody you need to call long distance and say, "Brother, I know there has been a wall between us, but I forgive you, and I want you to know that."

When you come to the cross, it is not some fine-spun theological theory to argue about. The cross is not some theological football to kick back and forth. When I come to Jesus and see how He forgives me, He pours that forgiveness into my life for other people. The cross makes the difference.

2. The cross reveals the enormity—the depth—of God's love.

It leads us to a deeper lesson of love than the human mind can fathom or experience. In one of the most profound passages in the New Testament, Paul puts it this way:

> "For he [that is, God] hath made him [that is, Christ] to be sin for us, who knew no sin; that we might be made the righteousness of God in him." 2 Corinthians 5:21.

God made Christ to be sin for us. Did Jesus ever sin? Did He ever think an evil thought? Did He ever commit a selfish act? Certainly not. But He who knew no sin, became sin.

What does it mean that Christ became sin for us? What are these deeper lessons of the cross that—once we understand them—transform our thinking and change our entire being? Why did Jesus Himself say, "If I be lifted up, I will draw all men unto Me"? John 12:32. Why is it that the cross breaks the habits of sin in our lives? Why is it that the cross transforms us? Why is it that the cross can make a dishonest man honest? An impure man or woman pure? An angry man patient? How does the cross break the grip and hold of sin in the life?

We don't need so much a theological definition as we need to understand the practical realities of the cross. Our great need is to experience its transforming power. What is this deeper meaning of the love of God in the cross? Understanding what Jesus really suffered helps us comprehend its deeper message. Paul reveals that depth in these words: "Christ has redeemed us from the curse of the law, being made a curse for us: for it is written, 'Cursed is every one that hangeth on a tree.'" Galatians 3:13.

Christ has redeemed us from the curse of the law. What is the curse of the law? Death. Is it the first death—or the second death? Well, let's define these terms. The first death is the death that the entire human race dies as the result of the corporate sin of humanity. When Adam and Eve sinned, this world was plunged into death and separated from God. God is the source of life, and as the result of being separated from Him through sin—just as a branch broken off from an apple tree has no life—all of us are separated from the source of life and experience the first or physical death.

Now, if the death of Christ on the cross is only for our physical death, we have no salvation, because sin also necessitates the second death, which is banishment forever from the presence of God. It is an unconscious state that lasts forever. After the agony of God's judgment as the result of sin, after the punishment which comes at the end of time, the second death is eternal separation—eternal banishment from the presence of God.

The author of Hebrews says that Christ tasted death for every human being (see Hebrews 2:8). When He died on the cross, He died not merely the first death, but He experienced eternal separation from God as the result of sin. He experienced the guilt of sin and was willing to be eternally banished from God. The question is, "When did Christ experience this?"

Did Christ experience the second death before He died—or after He died? Well, if you say that it was after He died, then that must mean there is some consciousness after death. Is there any consciousness after death? "The living know that they shall die, but the dead know not anything." Ecclesiastes 9:5. So, if Christ is to experience the second death, He has to experience it, not after He dies, but in the conscious moments before He dies.

From twelve o'clock to three o'clock, during those final hours of darkness when Christ hung on the cross, He especially bore the accumulated guilt of the sins of the world. During those hours, Christ voluntarily accepted the corporate guilt of humanity. During those hours from twelve to three o'clock, Christ could not see through the darkness, and He experienced separation from the Father. If we define the second death as eternal banishment from the presence of the Father, and if we define the second death as God's judgment against sin, then for three hours as Christ hung on the cross—in His conscious moments—He could not see Himself ever being reconciled to the Father again. Christ was willing to go into the grave. He was willing to go into the tomb and never, ever, come out if that meant that you could be in heaven with the Father.

As Jesus hung on the cross, He thought about His relationship with His Father. He considered His oneness with the Father from eternity. Who is this who is dying? Who is this who has nails through His hands? Who is this who has blood running down His face? Who is this with agony in His eyes? It is Jesus—the one at whose command angels wing their way to worlds afar. Who is this who suffers so? It is Jesus—the one at the mention of whose very name angels sing, "Holy, Holy, Holy." Who is this who suffers so? He is the one worshiped by cherubim and seraphim. He is the one who spoke and worlds came into existence. He is the one whose very word created Earth from nothing. He is the one who carpeted Earth with green—the one who caused streams to babble and flow, birds to sing, fruit trees to blossom, and flowers to spring up. Who is this who suffers? He is Jesus—the one who existed with the Father from eternity.

I travel a lot in my work, and I have a fifteen-year-old son. When I have been on an overseas trip and I get back, I look forward to seeing my boy. My wife often brings him to the airport, and sometimes when I come through passport control, I see that little guy. We are great friends. Sometimes I see him look up at my wife and say, "Ma, there's Dad!" As I move through the crowd, we embrace as we greet one another. If I thought that I had to be separated from my son forever, and never, ever see him again, it would break my heart.

But Jesus had a much closer relationship with His Father than I have with my son. Christ—the fountain of love, the essence of love—entered the tomb without knowling that He would be with the Father forever. He was willing to go to the tomb so that we could sit upon the throne. He died committing His life into the Father's hands, willing to bear sin's penalty in His own body, to save us. For Jesus, the knowledge that we would be in heaven made His death worth it all. I will never fully understand that love or comprehend it. All I can do is to go to my knees and give Him my heart. All I can do, in the light of Calvary's love, is to say, "Father, I am Yours."

The habits of sin have no hold when you see Calvary's love. True, you may fail. True, you may have times in your life when you fall short. But once you look into the eyes of a man who loved and cared for you so much that He would have gone into the grave so that you could go to heaven, you can only respond in gratitude. All you can do is open your heart to appreciate it and accept it. And that love breaks the chains of sin. That love makes you a new man—it makes you a new woman.

3. The cross reveals that you are worth something.

The cross says that you are not just a speck of cosmic dust. You are not merely skin covering bones. You are not simply some genetic accident. The cross says that you are not just an enlarged protein molecule. The cross reveals the magnitude of God's forgiveness. The cross reveals the enormity of God's love. The cross says, "Lift up your head—you are worth something."

You are not merely one of the billions of people on Planet Earth. You are not merely a rock or a pebble or a run-over Pepsi can. You are not some smashed Coke bottle by the side of the road. You have worth in God's sight.

I love the way Paul puts it so personally:

> "I am crucified with Christ: nevertheless I live; yet not I, but Christ liveth in me: and the life that I now live in the flesh I live by the faith of the Son of God, who loved me, and gave Himself for me." Galatians 2:20.

You may say, "I can't understand that. How in the world does Jesus even know I exist? I mean, really now, there are over five billion people clawing at one another for living space on Planet Earth. How do I make any difference? God has all those angels, so really now, does it really make any difference whether I am saved or lost?"

There is a place in God's heart just for you. There is an emptiness in His heart only you can fill. If you are lost, He will be lonely for you throughout eternity. Now, somebody says, "That's nice to say, Mark, but it is just not real."

Maybe this illustration will help you. Are you a parent? Do you have more than one child? Let's suppose you have nine children. Johnny is seven years old, and he is out kicking a soccer ball in the front yard, and you are sitting on the front porch watching him. Johnny kicks the ball out into the road.

Now, as he is running to get the ball, you see a car coming down the street, and you shout, "Johnny, Johnny—the car!" But Johnny doesn't see the car, and it hits him. The car runs him over, and Johnny is dead.

The day of the funeral is coming, and the pastor and I decide to visit you in hopes of bringing you some comfort. And I say to the pastor, "Now, don't worry about this too much. Let me take over this situation and give the counsel." And he replies, "Well, OK. Do you have a plan?"

"Oh, yes, I have a plan. It is a sure-fire plan to help this couple through their mourning and grief and agony. What we really need to do is show them all the benefits of Johnny's death. Here is the approach. After entering the house, I will make a comment something like this, 'You know, I am sorry that Johnny died, but I thought that really, to help you it would be better to think about all the benefits of his death. You know, this will save you over $9,000 a year in college expenses, and you can go on vacation with that extra money.

"And I was thinking too, that when you have ice cream for dessert, you can all get a ninth more this way. And you only have to buy eight pairs of shoes now instead of nine. Also, you will now have a ninth more time. Another thing I was thinking is that I have two girls and one boy—three children—and that necessitates a lot of time. You have eight, and think of how blessed you are. You will hardly have time to miss Johnny.'"

What the family would say to me is, "All the eight don't replace Johnny." They would say, "There is a special place in our hearts only for him. All eight of our children, whom we love dearly, don't make up for the one that is missing. Our hearts long for him."

And the infinite God who gives moms and dads the ability to love three, five, seven, or eight has the ability to love more than one child—He has the ability to love billions. Yet there is a place in His heart just for you. And there is nobody else like you in the universe.

The cross says, "You are special." In the heart of this preacher, there are ups and there are downs. There are times that I get discouraged. Sometimes, in those quiet times, I think about that cross, and I think about that Lord, and I hear Him whisper, "You are special. You mean something to me. I am concerned about your problems. I am concerned about your heartaches. I am concerned about your burdens."

Lift up your head, brother. Lift up your head, sister. You are special to God. There is a place in His heart only for you. Look to the cross. Look at those outstretched arms and hear Him say to you, "My child, my death was for you. I long for you to be in heaven. I want you to be with me there, forever."

4. The cross reveals hope in despair.

It was Friday—a dark, dark Friday. They nailed Him to the cross on Friday. They put a crown of thorns on His head on Friday. They put a spear wound in His side on Friday. The sun veiled its face on Friday. The earth quaked on Friday. The birds stopped singing on Friday. It thundered and the sky was laced with lightning on Friday. Judas betrayed Him on Friday. Peter forsook Him on Friday. The disciples fled on Friday. On an old, rugged cross on a dirt hill outside of Jerusalem, the Son of God died on a Friday. It was a dark, dark Friday.

But resurrection morning was coming. And beyond the rejection and betrayal and despair, beyond the blood and agony and tears, beyond the brokenness and disappointment and despair, was resurrection morning.

And the sun rose on resurrection morning—and the birds sang on resurrection morning. The voice of God spoke on resurrection morning. "Son, Thy Father calleth Thee." And all the Roman soldiers could not keep Him in the tomb. The stone sealing the tomb rolled away like a pebble. In glory and splendor, the Son of God came forth anew! There is hope in despair, because although there was a crucifixion on Friday, there was a resurrection on Sunday morning. There is joy in the morning.

My brother, my sister, you may be going through despair right now. You may be going through heartache. You may be going through the agony of a divorce. You may be going through economic difficulty. There may be cancer cells in your body—I don't know what physical pain you may be going through. I don't know what sorrows you may be experiencing. I wish I did know.

Some of you carry real and heavy burdens. You brought your children up in church, but now they are gone. They have no interest in religion. Some of you carry burdens of guilt—some are depressed and discouraged. And the problems of your life are so big and you are so burdened down by them that it is difficult to see through them. Hang on, brother! Hang on, sister! There is joy in the morning!

In Tehran, Iran, is a beautiful, magnificent Muslim mosque. When you walk into the foyer of that mosque, it has marble columns, and as the sun shines through a translucent roof and sparkles in the atrium filled with plants, it looks as if you are standing in the middle of diamonds.

The story of the building of that mosque is fascinating. The cut mirrors cost literally tens of thousands of dollars and were made in Italy. They were flown into the airport in Tehran, but while they were being transported to the work site, all of these mirrors were broken. When they arrived at the work site, they were cracked. The workmen were so disappointed and discouraged that they were going to throw them away.

But one master artist examined them. He took a hammer and began to crack the mirrors even further. He took the jagged pieces of glass and placed each piece carefully into a wet cement wall. Today those broken mirror fragments reflect the sun like acres of diamonds. The atrium is more beautiful than can possibly be imagined. The mirrors were broken— only to be made more beautiful.

Bring your brokenness to the cross. Bring your burdens to the cross. For at the cross, you find forgiveness and deliverance from guilt. At the cross, you find mercy and the ability to forgive. At the cross, the love of God breaks the hard-hearted habits of sin in your life, and there at the cross, you can give yourself away. At the cross, you will sense that you are worth something. You are emphatically not some speck of cosmic dust. At the cross, Jesus says, "I care for you. Whatever your despair or your problem, here is hope." At the cross, you will be drawn nearer and nearer to Him.

Someone reading these words has heard the voice of God speaking to you. You may have been burdened with a load of guilt, and you want to be a different man—a different woman. Christ speaks to you right now from the cross and says, "Come unto me all that are burdened and heavy laden, and I will give you rest."

You can find forgiveness now. You can find freedom from guilt now at the cross. Perhaps you carry a load of bitterness because someone has treated you unjustly or wrongly, and you want to leave all this at the foot of the cross. Perhaps you are wrestling with giant problems in your life. And you have been discouraged because these problems have looked so big. Problems in your marriage. Problems with your health. Leave them at the foot of the cross right now! At the cross, there is mercy and forgiveness. At the cross, there is hope in despair. Bring it all to Jesus.

Miracle of miracles! Jesus knows why you have come to Him. He knows every thought of your heart. Christianity is not some game. It is not some make-believe phenomenon. There is a real God and a real Jesus. He is concerned about you. He knows your problems and your difficulties. Right now, from the sanctuary above, He sends angels to your side, because He cares so much for you—because you mean so much to Him. Right now, your name is on His lips, and He is presenting your name before the Father in heaven. And right now, He imparts to you peace, joy, assurance, and the knowledge that you are His.

6

The Night Jesus Prayed for You

On an April day in the early 1900s, the famed *Titanic* sped toward New York. No one knew that it was to be the *Titanic*'s last journey! When the huge ship hit an iceberg with its engines at full throttle, a large, gaping hole was ripped in its hull. The massive liner slowly began to sink beneath the waves. Then, in an instant, it was gone. Over fifteen hundred people died that fateful evening. Many fascinating human-interest stories have emerged from that tragedy.

One story that has deeply impressed me is that of a little-known man by the name of Colonel Gacey. Colonel Gacey's wife couldn't sleep the night of the *Titanic*'s voyage. She was thousands of miles from the location of the tragedy in the North Atlantic. As she anxiously awaited her husband's arrival from Liverpool, England, on the *Titanic*, she experienced a strange sense of foreboding. She was restless— sleep would not come.

Early in the morning, she awoke to pray. Little did she know that the *Titanic*, carrying her husband, had hit an iceberg and was going down. Little did she know that her husband had leaped overboard into the icy waters of the Atlantic and was struggling for his life. In the early hours of the morning, a strange peace came over Mrs. Gacey. Later she commented, "It was as if the arms of God encircled me. I climbed back into bed and fell asleep."

Precisely at that hour, her husband, thousands of miles away, was struggling for his life in the icy waters of the Atlantic. Freezing, he thought, "This is it—life is over." Just when he could hold on no longer, a lifeboat appeared out of nowhere. Desperately, he grasped the side of the boat. Strong arms pulled him aboard. God does answer prayer. It is thrilling for a husband to know that his wife is praying for him.

Blessed is that man whose wife knows God and prays for him. Blessed is that woman whose husband knows God and prays for her. Blessed are those young people whose parents know God and pray for them.

I went through some rocky years as a teenager. Sports had become my god. I was looking for meaning and purpose in life. I remember Friday nights when I was sixteen years old. I certainly was not a committed Christian. I liked to watch the late, late, late Friday night shows. I remember sitting in the living room watching Dracula movies. For some reason they attracted me. I don't know why, as I look back on it now. Frankenstein was a close second, and Alfred Hitchcock ranked in my top-ten list, as well.

I had little interest in my father's religion back then. But I remember on those late Friday nights looking through a crack in the door of the small den next to the TV room. And I remember seeing my father with his Bible on his lap. From time to time, he dropped to his knees by the side of his old favorite chair, and I listened to the echo of his prayers. "Dear God, please bless my boy. Keep him safe and secure. Lead him to Jesus." And in my teen years, the echoes of my dad's prayers kept me from doing some things that I know I would have done without those prayers.

Blessed is that husband whose wife is praying for him. Blessed is that wife whose husband is praying for her. Blessed are teenagers during those traumatic years of their lives who sense that their parents know God and are praying for them.

It is one thing to have your father or mother praying for you. It's encouraging to know that your husband or your wife is praying for you. But it is even more reassuring to know that Christ is praying for you.

John 17 is one of the most significant chapters in the Bible. It records Jesus' most comprehensive prayer for His people. In this chapter we listen to Jesus' earnest longing for His people to be saved. Jesus Christ focused His attention in prayer on you. Before Him lay Pilate's judgment hall, the whip and the lash, and Golgatha's hill. Before Him were the cruel nails which would pierce tender flesh, the crown of thorns which would be jammed upon His head, and the spear which would wound His side. Before Him was the mockery of the trial, rejection by the Jews, and the ridicule of His own people. Nevertheless, that night in the garden, Jesus was praying for you. He looked beyond Pilate's judgment hall, beyond Golgatha's hill—and He thought of you.

His prayer speaks to us of the greatest love in all the universe. "These words spake Jesus and lifted up his eyes to heaven and said, 'Father, the hour is come. Glorify thy Son that thy Son may also glorify thee.'" John 17:1. "Father, the hour is come" . . . the hour to which millions through time have looked forward . . . the hour that the searchlight of history has focused upon . . . the hour that the prophets have proclaimed . . . the hour for which the hearts of men and women through generations have waited. Father, that hour has come—the hour of my death and the cross, the hour when the controversy between good and evil will be finally and fully settled as the Son of God offers His life as a sacrifice on Calvary's cross.

"Father, the hour is come. Glorify thy Son, that thy Son also may glorify thee." The hour of Jesus' greatest agony was the hour of His greatest glory. The hour of His death was the hour of His glorification. Jesus marched to death, not as a defeated soldier, but as a conquering general. The hour of Christ's death was to be the hour of His greatest glory, because it was the clearest demonstration in the universe of a Father's love. Jesus revealed His matchless love on the cross. Never again would there be any justification for doubting that love. Never again would the human race have any possible reason to misunderstand that love. Never again would human beings have any reason to place a low value upon themselves. The cross demonstrated before a waiting world and a watching universe the magnificence of God's love.

There is a fascinating painting in the Washington

Art Gallery. In a moving World War II scene, the artist depicts a battlefield with two groups of tanks moving toward one another. Two divisions of Allied forces are attacking the Nazi forces. The tanks are firing their guns. Ground troops are in full battle. One lone soldier in the center of the picture captures your attention. Two groups of Allied soldiers have been cut off from one another. An enemy bullet has pierced their telephone communication line. In the midst of heavy gunfire, a lone soldier is responsible for repairing the severed phone lines. His hands are outstretched over his head as he works on the wire.

Just as he completes the job, bullets rip through his uniform. His chest is spattered with blood. The artist has chosen one word to describe the picture. The word that describes the scene is "Through." The message of the picture is obvious—a lone soldier gave his life; his blood-spattered uniform indicates that the message got through. Communication is reestablished!

When Jesus Christ was lifted high on a cross above Jerusalem, He got the message through. Satan is a liar. God is love. Divine love would go to any length to save the human race. The prayer of Jesus that night in John 17 is saturated with love. Calvary's mountain echoes love through the valleys of earth. Jesus looked beyond Pilate's judgment hall, beyond Gethsemane's garden, beyond the farce of the trial, and beyond Calvary's mountain. He looked ahead to the trials and temptations, the suffering and sorrow, the disappointments and discouragement His followers would face throughout the centuries. He was going home, but His followers would still be in this world.

Jesus made three specific requests for us that

night! "Holy Father, keep through thine own name those whom thou hast given me, that they may be one, as we are." John 17:11. Jesus was thinking about you. He wasn't thinking about the crown or the nails or the spear that night—He was thinking about you. He was not thinking about Himself but about His church.

"That they all may be one; as thou, Father, art in me, and I in thee, that they also may be one in us: that the world may believe that thou hast sent me." John 17:21.

He prayed for the unity of His church. He prayed for oneness and harmony. He was going to leave His followers. He was leaving a small band of disciples with a variety of temperaments, with different dispositions and attitudes. He thought of Peter who was so outspoken, of Matthew who was so exacting, of Thomas who tended to doubt, of Philip who was introverted and reflective, and John who had a fiery temper.

As Jesus thought of these men with such different backgrounds and dispositions, He thought of the church in all ages and prayed, "Father, with their different backgrounds, with their different dispositions, with their diverse ways of looking at things, Father, keep them as one."

The most convincing evidence that Jesus came into the world is the loving unity among His followers of varied backgrounds. The greatest testimonies to the power of the gospel are not fine church buildings or magnificent institutions. The world knows how to construct buildings and marvelous edifices. But the most convincing evidence that Jesus Christ has come into the world is to be seen in the transformations that take place in the hearts and lives of people.

Jesus prayed for oneness among His followers. He prayed that husbands and wives would be one. He prayed that there would be a sweet, loving spirit in our homes. He prayed that parents would be one with their children. He prayed that children would be one with their parents—that they all might be one. "That the world may know that thou hast sent me."

He prayed that there would be oneness on the nominating committee and on the church board. He prayed that there would be oneness on the school board. He prayed that there would be unity and harmony in the institution.

And when I am prone to push my own way and to allow my ego to selfishly assert my own opinion . . . when I am prone to break up unity and harmony with my wife and my children . . . when I am prone to push my own way on the church board or the school board . . . when I am tempted by the accuser of the brethren to criticize and gossip and cut down a church member with my tongue . . . I remember a garden. I remember a night with Jesus on His knees, praying that the church would be one and that there would be love and unity—brother holding the hand of brother and sister holding the hand of sister— and that through that loving atmosphere of fellowship, unbelievers would come to see Christ.

The echoes of that prayer of Jesus reverberate down the corridor of time and speak to my heart as I listen to Him pray, "Father, that they all may be one. That the world may know that thou hast sent me."

Jesus prayed first that His church be one. That night He was thinking about you. That night, your home was in His mind. Your husband, your wife, was in His mind. Your children were in His mind.

That night, your church was in His mind. But then His prayer continues.

Earnestly petitioning the Father, He declared, "I pray not that thou shouldest take them out of the world, but that thou shouldest keep them from the evil. They are not of the world, even as I am not of the world. Sanctify them through thy truth: thy word is truth." John 17:15-17.

Jesus was saying, "I do not pray that my followers separate themselves from the world in high-walled monasteries. There will be temptation all around them. They will be enticed to do evil. The attractions of sin will be very real to them. Satan's temptations are not make-believe—they will be tempted on every hand. They will be enticed to forget me. Their priorities may become confused. Father, I pray not that You take them out of the world. I pray that in the midst of Satan's fiercest temptations, through the sanctifying influence of my Word, their hearts and minds will be transformed. Father, I pray that through my Word, their minds will be protected from the evil of the world."

Many books are inspiring, but the Bible is inspired. Many books are enlightening, but the Bible is enlightened. Many books are food for the mind, but the Bible is food for the soul. Many books provide a direction for life, but the Bible provides a power for living.

Jesus was saying, "In the merry-go-round of life, when values are distorted and priorities are confused—in a world where down is up and up is down, in a world that has confused its price tags—fill your mind with truths from the Word of God."

And when life gets busy and my priorities are mixed up, I remember a garden and I remember a night. When I am tempted to rush headlong into the day forgetting those still, small moments with God in prayer, when I am tempted to allow dust to gather on the Book, when I am inclined to face the tempter in my own strength, I remember a garden and I remember a night. I listen to the echoes of the words of Jesus, "Sanctify them through thy truth," and I open the pages of the sacred Book to find meaning and strength to live in the nineties.

Jesus prayed first for the unity of His church. He prayed second that men and women on the merry-go-round of the nineties, with life whirling by at its hectic pace, would not forget what really counts for eternity. He prayed that they would allow His Word to sanctify them as they spend time reading its pages.

Finally, Jesus reaches the climax of His prayer. In John 17:24, Jesus prays,

"Father, I will that they also, whom thou hast given me, be with me where I am: that they may behold my glory, which thou hast given me: for thou lovest me before the foundation of the world."

Think of what Jesus was facing. Yet He was not thinking of His suffering, pain, and agony. His mind was not filled with what would happen to Him. He was thinking about you. He was thinking about me. Christ knew that beyond the suffering, beyond the rejection, beyond the death, there was a resurrection morning. Jesus knew that soon He would be going home.

Volumes have been written about the birth of Jesus. Scores of books have been written about the life of Christ—tens of thousands of pages. Much has been written about the death of Christ and about His resurrection and second coming. But little has been written or preached about the homecoming of Jesus Christ. Jesus was getting ready to go home. He had been in this world for thirty-three and a half years.

Think of it! Christ had been separated from His Father for all those years. The infinite Christ, with an infinite capacity to love, had existed in heaven from all eternity in loving harmony and absolute oneness with His Father. For millions and billions and trillions of years, the self-existing Christ had never been separated from the Father. At a given moment in time—at a specific date in history—Christ plunged into the arena of human affairs, taking on the form of man.

For the first time, He was separated from His Father. From the very dawning of His human intelligence, He consciously sensed that separation. Yes, He spent time in prayer. Yes, He spent time in devotion. But He was nonetheless separated from His Father for thirty-three and a half years. I don't know about you, but when I think about that separation, I can identify with it just a bit, even though it is hard fully to comprehend.

Since I travel a great deal in my ministry as an international television speaker and evangelist, I am away from my family for significant periods of time. Separation isn't easy for me. It is a painful experience because of the love that exists in our family. But that separation hardly compares to the separation of Jesus from His Father for thirty-three and a half years.

Have you ever been away from someone you loved—someone you loved immensely and dearly—for six months, a year, two years? For thirty-three and a half years, one who was loved, who came on a mission of love, who embodied everything love stands for, was wrenchingly separated from His Father. He was separated from His Father's immense love for thirty-three and a half years. And now, after the farce of a trial, after enduring the jeering mockery of the crowd and a painful and agonizing crucifixion, after a glorious and triumphant resurrection, it was time for Jesus to go home.

On the Mount of Olives, He lifts His hands in blessing on His disciples. He is going home now; it is time to leave. And as He lifts His hands, a force greater than the launching power of a thousand rockets, a force greater than the force of gravity, begins to draw Him heavenward. He is going home now.

Man steps off a mountain and goes down. God steps off a mountain and goes up. The Creator is greater than the laws of His creation. He begins to ascend from earth to heaven. As the sun illuminates the deep blue sky and puffy white clouds hang over the Galilean landscape, He is going home.

As He ascends higher and higher, He looks down and sees His disciples standing there. He sees the Sea of Galilee upon which He once walked. He sees Bethlehem and remembers how He was born there in a wooden cradle. He sees Calvary, where He was nailed to a wooden cross. He sees Pilate's judgment hall, where He was condemned. He sees the Mount of Olives, where He gave His magnificent sermons. He sees Bethany, the home of Mary and Martha and Lazarus. He sees the empty tomb of Lazarus, and as He ascends higher still, He sees His own empty tomb in the garden, with the stone rolled away.

He is going home. Soon He is out of sight of earth and within sight of heaven. As He ascends, He is met by tens of thousands of angelic beings. The Bible records the chorus the angels sing as they meet their returning Lord. David pictures the scene in Psalm 24. He describes its beauty and majesty. The psalmist pictures this grand and glorious occasion as Jesus is returning home. In majesty and glory and splendor, He is met by angels who begin to sing in chorus—a great antiphonal chorus.

The angels divide into two groups. One group sings the melody, asking a question—and the other sings a harmonious response. The combined voices of countless angels reverberate throughout all heaven. "Lift up your heads,O ye gates, and be ye lift up, ye everlasting doors; and the King of glory shall come in." Psalm 24:7-10.

Listen as one group of angels asks in song, "Who is this King of glory?" And another group responds, "The Lord strong and mighty, the Lord mighty in battle." They do not ask, "Who is this King of Glory?" because they do not know. They repeat the musical question because they want to sing praises to His name.

The angels desire to sing, "Worthy, worthy is the Lamb that was slain. to receive riches, and honor, and power, and glory forever." They want to praise his name—the King is coming home. The joyous song echoes and reechoes through the chambers of heaven: "Lift up your heads, O ye gates; even lift them up, ye everlasting doors; and the King of glory shall come in. Who is this King of glory? The Lord of hosts, He is the King of glory."

The gates of heaven swing open and, surrounded by the rapturous singing of tens of thousands of adoring angels, Jesus Christ enters into the glorious splendor of heaven. And there, standing before Him with arms wide open, is His Father. In that magnificent moment, Father and Son are reunited. As they approach one another in the ecstasy of the moment, a hush falls over heaven. Seraphim and cherubim are silent. The angel hosts are quiet now.

The angels prepare to lift their voices again in a rapturous song of praise. But Jesus raises His hands and waves them back. He stands silent before His Father for a moment. Jesus will not yet accept the adoration of the angels. He will not yet accept the warm embrace of the Father. Jesus stands and lifts His nail-scarred hands and says, "Father, I will that those whom thou hast given me be with me where I am. Father, I cannot accept Your warm embrace or the praise of the angels until I know that because of Calvary's cross, because of my sacrifice, my followers on earth will be here with me someday." And the Father replies, "Son, the sacrifice is accepted." Immediately the angels strike again the chorus, "Worthy, worthy is the Lamb that was slain."

If that night in the garden—with Pilate's judgment hall and Calvary's mountain before Him, with the nails, the whip, the crown of thorns, and the cross before Him—Jesus thought enough of me to pray for me, He must love me a great deal. And if Jesus that long-ago day in heaven would not accept the embrace of the Father—the loving squeeze of His heavenly Dad—until He knew that I would be there, then if He loves me that much, I want to be there!

When life seems to have little meaning and your head seems to be spinning, when discouragement crashes in on you like waves, when despondency overwhelms you, remember a garden, remember a night, and listen to the echo of the words of Christ, "Father, I will that they be with me where I am."

Remember, Jesus is praying for you! Allow the echoes of His prayer to inspire you not to give up.

If Jesus is praying for you, you can make it, friend. Never give up! Never surrender to Satan's temptations to discouragement. Jesus is praying for you! You can be saved! You can live in heaven forever! He wants you to be there.

There is power in the prayers of Jesus. He prayed for you in the garden that night. He thought of you when He hung on Calvary's cross. Before He accepted the throne in heaven again, He wanted the assurance that you would be there—and He is praying for you today.

Praise His holy name!